Outstanding Dissertations in
ECONOMICS

A Continuing Garland Research Series

The Efficiency of Private Antitrust Enforcement
The "Illinois Brick" Decision

Valerie Sarris

Garland Publishing, Inc.
New York & London, 1984

Valerie Sarris © 1984
All rights reserved

Library of Congress Cataloging in Publication Data

Sarris, Valerie, 1951–
    The efficiency of private antitrust enforcement.

  (Outstanding dissertations in economics)
  Originally presented as the author's thesis (doctoral)—Yale University, 1979.
  Bibliography: p.
    1. Antitrust law—United States. I. Title. II. Series.
KF1657.T7S27 1984   343.73'072   79-53645
ISBN 0-8240-4163-1   347.30372

All volumes in this series are printed on acid-free, 250-year-life paper.

Printed in the United States of America

THE EFFICIENCY OF PRIVATE ANTITRUST ENFORCEMENT;

THE ILLINOIS BRICK DECISION AND ITS IMPLICATIONS

A Dissertation

Presented to the Faculty of the Graduate School

of

Yale University

in Candidacy for the Degree of

Doctor of Philosophy

Valerie Sarris

1979

ACKNOWLEDGMENTS

I would like to express my sincere appreciation to the three members of my thesis committee, Professors Merton Peck, Richard Levin, and Sidney Winter for their advice and guidance during the completion of this dissertation.

The chairman of my committee, Professor Merton J. Peck first sparked my interest in private antitrust enforcement in his Industrial Organization class during my first year of graduate school. I am indebted to him for his helpful suggestions which enabled me to integrate my narrow focus with his broader perspective.

Professor Richard Levin was an invaluable source of both inspiration and extremely helpful criticism throughout the entire dissertation writing process. I wish to take this opportunity to express my appreciation for his painstakingly thorough comments and suggestions.

I am thankful to Professor Sidney Winter who offered helpful suggestions toward improving the models in both Chapters II and III.

The empirical portions of this dissertation would not have been possible without the cooperation I received from the legal community. I owe great thanks to the many state antitrust directors who generously agreed to answer my questionnaire. In particular I'd like to thank Charlie Brown, the antitrust director of the state of West Virginia, for his assistance in improving the response rate of the survey, and William Eskridge for his many helpful suggestions.

I am greatly indebted to Jeff Strnad, not only for his legal advice, but more importantly for the moral support he continually provided, particularly during those times when completion seemed like an impossible dream.

Last but not least, I would like to thank Glena Ames for her excellent typing job, and Eleanor van Buren for helping me get through graduate school.

TABLE OF CONTENTS

	page
LIST OF TABLES	vi
LIST OF FIGURES	vii

Chapter

I	INTRODUCTION	1
II	ANTITRUST AS A PUBLIC GOOD--PUBLIC OR PRIVATE PROVISION?	13
	I. Antitrust under Attack	14
	II. Antitrust--A Public Good	19
	III. A General Equilibrium Model of Antitrust Enforcement	22
	IV. The Spillover Effects of Public and Private Enforcement	40
	V. Breit and Elzinga--The Abolition of Private Antitrust	45
	VI. Public vs. Private--Which Is the More Efficient Enforcer?	53
III	PASSING-ON IN THEORY AND FACT--WHO BEARS THE BURDEN OF THE OVERCHARGE?	65
	I. In Defense of a Partial Equilibrium Framework	68
	II. Simple Monopoly Case	69
	III. Competitive Direct Purchaser Markets	73
	IV. Oligopoly--Cournot Assumptions	76
	V. Oligopoly--Collusion	78
	VI. Input Substitutability	83
	VII. Price Fixed Good Not a Material Input	91
	VIII. Overcharge--A Burden to Other Factors of Production?	93
	IX. What if the Chain Were Longer?	96
	X. Who Is Injured?--Implications for Compensation	98

TABLE OF CONTENTS, continued

Chapter			Page
III	XI.	Implications for Compensation--General	104
	XII.	What if Compensation Were Unimportant?	107
		APPENDIX TO CHAPTER III	108
IV		ALTERNATIVES TO THE ILLINOIS BRICK RULE	116
	I.	Framework for the Solution to the Illinois Brick Problem--Efficiency and Compensation	117
	II.	The Illinois Brick Decision	123
	III.	Illinois Brick--A Necessary Consequence of Hanover Shoe?	125
	IV.	The Advantages and Disadvantages of Illinois Brick	128
	V.	Why Direct Purchasers May Not Sue Their Suppliers	133
	VI.	A Proposal to Amend the Statute of Limitations	135
	VII.	Other Possible Solutions to the Illinois Brick Dilemma	140
V		THE ADMINISTRATIVE COSTS OF ENFORCEMENT	144
	I.	Complexity and Manageability of Antitrust Litigation	146
	II.	Multiple Liability	160
	III.	State Attorneys General--The New Enforcers	163
VI		WHO SUES THE PRICE FIXER?	174
	I.	Who Sues the Price Fixer?--Casual Evidence	177
	II.	Case by Case Approach	184
	III.	Another Approach	193
	IV.	Survey Results	201
VII		CONCLUSION	214
BIBLIOGRAPHY			226
TABLE OF CASES			228

LIST OF TABLES

Table   Page

Chapter III

Table 1   The Effect of the Elasticity of Substitution on the Cost of Output, $\alpha = 1/2$ 89

Table 2   The Effect of the Elasticity of Substitution on the Cost of Output, $\alpha = .2, .8$ 90

Table 3   Department of Justice Price Fixing Cases   101

CHAPTER VI

Table 1   Treble Damage Cases   203

LIST OF FIGURES

Figure   Page

Chapter II

Figure 1   The Antitrust Violations Market----------------------------- 30

Figure 2   A Family of Isowelfare Cost Curves----------------------- 31

Figure 3   The Effect of an Increase in Penalties--A Reduction
              in the Number of Violations and an Unknown Change
              in the Number of Suits------------------------------------ 32

Figures 4, 5 The Effects of an Increase in Penalties When the
              Costs of Suit May Vary------------------------------------ 34

Figure 6   The Effect of a Decrease in the Costs of Suit----------- 35

Figure 7   The Effect of a Decrease in the Costs of Suit--
              Defendants Are Myopic------------------------------------- 36

Figure 8   The Effect of a Decrease in the Costs of Suit--
              An Example Where Society Is Worse Off-------------------- 37

Figure 9   The Effect of an Increased Number of Plaintiffs--------- 38

Figure 10   The Effect of Class Actions------------------------------ 39

Figure 11   An Illustration of Overenforcement---------------------- 52

Chapter III

Figure 1   The Extent of Passing on in a Competitive Industry------ 73

Figure 2   Dominant Firm Profit Maximization----------------------- 80

Chapter VI

Figure 1   Deterrence Cannot be Inferred from Numbers of Suits----- 176

CHAPTER I

INTRODUCTION

On June 9, 1977, the Supreme Court of the United States announced a decision having considerable potential impact on the private enforcement of the antitrust laws. In <u>Illinois Brick</u> v. <u>State of Illinois</u>[1] the Court ruled on a treble damage action brought by the State of Illinois and numerous local governmental entities against the Illinois Brick Co. and other manufacturers of concrete blocks for damages pursuant to an alleged price fixing conspiracy. The Court ruled that <u>as a matter of law</u> the plaintiffs could not bring suit against the concrete block manufacturers because they had not purchased the price fixed goods directly from the price fixer, but instead purchased the concrete blocks through two layers of contractors who incorporated the blocks into buildings. In light of the recognized importance of private litigants in enforcing the antitrust laws, and of the large proportion of total recoveries collected by indirect purchaser plaintiffs, an investigation of the economic implications of <u>Illinois Brick</u> seems in order. The central question to be addressed by this dissertation is whether the direct purchaser rule articulated in <u>Illinois Brick</u> or some other combination of rules and procedures would best promote the public

---

[1] 431 U.S. 720.

policy goals underlying the antitrust laws. This chapter first provides a brief factual background to private enforcement in general and Illinois Brick in particular. Following this an outline of the entire dissertation is discussed.

Public and Private Enforcement--Treble Damages

The antitrust laws of the United States are enforced both by public agencies and by private parties who are injured by antitrust violations. These public agencies, the Antitrust Division of the Department of Justice and the Federal Trade Commission, may bring civil or criminal suits[2] against suspected violators for injunctive relief, the payment of fines, and more infrequently prison sentences and structural changes. In the same statutes in which Congress provided for public antitrust enforcement, an explicit means of private remedy was provided. In section 4 of the Clayton Antitrust Act which amended section 7 of the Sherman Act the Congress legislated that:

> Any person who shall be injured in his business or property by reason of anything forbidden in the antitrust laws may sue therefor in any district court of the United States in the district in which the defendant resides or is found or has an agent, without respect to the amount in controversy, and shall recover threefold the damages by him sustained, and the cost of suit, including a reasonable attorney's fee.

This private remedy provides a companion to public enforcement for the dual purposes of further deterring antitrust violators and of compensating its victims. The Supreme Court in recent years has frequently expressed the importance of both these goals, compensation and deterrence,

---

[2] Only the Department of Justice may bring criminal suits.

to effective antitrust enforcement.[3] While the goals of compensation and deterrence seem to be generally accepted, considerable disagreement exists concerning the best means to attain these goals. This disagreement concerns two separate issues. The first and broader issue is the relative social efficiency of public versus private enforcement of the antitrust laws. The second issue concerns whether or not direct purchasers should have exclusive standing to sue in private antitrust suits. The next two sections describe the historical background leading to Illinois Brick and the decision itself.

Hanover Shoe and its Predessors

In Hanover Shoe v. United Shoe Machinery[4] the plaintiff, Hanover Shoe, a manufacturer of shoes, brought suit against United from whom it purchased shoe machinery. This antitrust treble damage action was filed pursuant to a 1954 monopoly conviction of the same defendant. United's defense was that Hanover was not "injured in his business or property" within the meaning of §4 because it had passed on the overcharge to its customers--the purchasers of shoes. In Hanover Shoe, the Court ruled that the passing on defense was impermissible as a matter of law and that the direct purchaser suing for treble damages was injured within the meaning of §4 for the full amount of the overcharge.

In Hanover Shoe, the Court reasoned first that it was unwilling to further complicate treble damage actions by tracing a cost increase

---

[3] See, e.g., Perma Life Mufflers, Inc. v. International Parts Co., 392 U.S. 134, 139 (1968), Brunswick Corp. v. Pueblo Bowl-O-Mat, Inc., 429 U.S. 477, 486 and Illinois Brick, 431 U.S. at 748 (Brennan, J., dissenting).

[4] 392 U.S. 481.

through several layers of a chain of distribution since this "would often require massive evidence and complicated theories."[5] In addition, the Court was concerned that absent the ability of direct purchasers to sue for the entire overcharge, antitrust violators "would retain the fruits of their illegality" since indirect purchasers "would have only a tiny stake in the lawsuit and hence little incentive to sue."[6] The Court delineated an exception to this direct purchaser rule in the case of a product which is sold pursuant to a pre-existing contract because it would then be easy to prove that the direct purchaser had not been injured. In making this exception the Court seemed to imply that the judicial burden argument was more important than the deterrence argument.

The Hanover Shoe decision was looked upon by many as a landmark in private antitrust enforcement. Prior to its announcement in 1960 (at the District Court level), passing on was considered to be a powerful defense for many alleged antitrust violators. During the pre-Hanover Shoe era, the applicability of the passing on defense often depended on what the plaintiff did with the price fixed item. If the item was resold without alteration (as by a middleman), the courts would usually accept the passing on defense, whereas if the direct purchaser was a consumer of the product (it used this product as an input in its own production process), the passing on defense was usually unavailable.[7] In the Oil Jobber Cases[8]

---

[5] 392 U.S. at 493.

[6] 392 U.S. at 494.

[7] Earl Pollock, "Automatic Treble Damages and the Passing on Defense," 13 Antitrust Bulletin 1183 (Winter 1968).

[8] See, e.g., Twin Ports Oil Co. v. Pure Oil Co., 119 F. 2d 747 (8th Cir. 1941), cert. denied, 314 U.S. 644 (1941). For other citations, see Pollock, p. 1194.

of the 1940's many gasoline distributors were denied recovery for failure to prove that they had not passed on to their service station customers the overcharges of the defendant oil companies. On the other hand, in Ohio Valley Electric Co. v. General Electric,[9] one of the electrical equipment conspiracy cases, the plaintiff recovered despite the fact that General Electric, a regulated public utility, passed on the overcharges to its customers. Hanover Shoe clearly erased the confusion concerning the availability of the defensive use of passing on and with it the middleman/consumer distinction by providing automatic recovery to any direct purchaser who could merely prove that he paid an overcharge. However, at the same time that it eliminated the ambiguities concerning the availability of the defensive use of passing on, it unleashed nine years of fresh confusion concerning the applicability of its holding to indirect purchaser plaintiffs. The question as to whether indirect purchasers could use passing on offensively remained unsettled until the announcement of the Illinois Brick decision in 1977.

Prior to the Illinois Brick announcement there was a split among the lower courts as to whether indirect purchasers could sue to collect treble damage recoveries or whether such a result was precluded as a matter of law because Hanover Shoe essentially provided for automatic recovery for direct purchasers. In the case of In re Western Liquid Asphalt Cases[10] a group of plaintiffs consisting primarily of state governments successfully sued producers of liquid asphalt for treble damages. The plaintiffs were indirect purchasers since they made purchases of roads and highways from paving contractors who themselves purchased asphalt directly from

---

[9] 244 F. Supp. 914 (S.D.N.Y. 1965).

[10] 487 F. 2d 191 (9th Cir. 1973), cert. denied, 415 U.S. 919 (1974).

the defendants. Yet, indirect purchasers of Plumbing Fixtures[11] by builders and owners of homes in which these fixtures were incorporated were thought to be too remote to be able to prove antitrust injury. In Illinois Brick the Supreme Court accepted certiorari in order to resolve the conflict among the various Circuit Courts of Appeal as to whether the offensive use of a passing on theory as used by indirect purchaser plaintiffs was consistent with Hanover Shoe.[12]

The Illinois Brick Decision

In Illinois Brick the State of Illinois and 700 local governmental entities brought an antitrust treble damage action against Illinois Brick and other manufacturers of concrete blocks, alleging that they were injured by illegal overcharges on the concrete blocks. Although the overcharges were paid directly by masonry contractors who were the direct purchasers from the defendant manufacturers, the plaintiffs contended that they were the ones truly injured by the antitrust violation since the overcharge was passed on to and hence borne by them.

Whereas in Hanover Shoe, the Court decided that the passing on theory may not be used defensively by an antitrust violator, Illinois Brick held that this theory may not be used offensively by an indirect purchaser plaintiff. The Supreme Court reached this decision in a series of steps. First it reasoned that whatever rule was adopted to govern the admissibility of passing on, it should be applied consistently to both plaintiff and defendant so as to avoid the possibility of multiple recovery.

---

[11] Philadelphia Housing Authority v. American Radiator and Standard Sanitary Corporation, 50 F.R.D. 13 (E.D. Pa. 1970).

[12] 420 U.S. at 728.

To allow the indirect purchaser plaintiff to attempt to prove that he had absorbed the overcharge while allowing the direct purchaser automatic recovery could possibly subject the defendant to double (or more for a longer chain of distribution) the treble damages intended by Congress. The Court was faced with the choice of denying recovery to indirect purchaser plaintiffs or of overruling (or narrowly limiting) the Hanover Shoe decision.

The Court reasoned that the uncertainties and difficulties encountered in analyzing price, output, cost, and demand conditions "in the real economic world rather than in the economist's hypothetical model"[13] applies no less to plaintiffs than to defendants attempting to prove that passing on has occurred. To allow indirect purchasers to assert that passing on has occurred may open the door to massive multiparty litigation which strains the ability of the courts to function effectively. Further, the Court reasoned, the objectives of antitrust enforcement would be better served by allowing the direct purchaser to sue for the entire overcharge than by attempting to apportion damages between a multitude of plaintiffs at various stages in the chain of distribution. Illinois Brick declined to carve out broad exceptions to its ruling for different types of markets, but instead left potential plaintiffs with two much more narrowly drawn exceptions: the cost plus contract, and the case where the direct purchaser is owned or controlled by its customer.

---

[13] Hanover Shoe 392 U.S. 481, 493.

Congressional Response to Illinois Brick

In direct response to the Illinois Brick decision, legislative proposals were immediately introduced into both Houses of Congress to effectively "repeal" both Hanover Shoe and Illinois Brick. In introducing the Senate bill, Senator Kennedy indicated that the majority opinion of Justice White was contrary to the clearly expressed will of Congress, as indicated both in the legislative history of the Sherman Act and the Congressional debate on the Hart-Scott-Rodino Antitrust Improvements Act of 1976. The Senate report on this bill, which in part provided that the state attorneys general could sue as parens patriae for damage done to its residents by reason of antitrust violations, concludes with the statement that "as between competing claimants within the chain of distribution ...including consumers, the section 4C(a)(1) proviso is intended to assure that the monetary relief is properly allocated."[14] Congressman Rodino was quoted as stating that "if the intervening presence of such a middleman is to prevent recovery, the bill will be utterly meaningless."[15] In the majority opinion Justice White indicated that of course "Congress is free to change this Court's interpretation of its legislation."[16] This is precisely what the sponsors of the legislation to overturn Illinois Brick intend to do.

By July of 1978, the Judiciary Committees of both Houses of Congress

---

[14] U.S., Congress, Senate, Committee on the Judiciary, Fair and Effective Enforcement of the Antitrust Laws, S. 1874, Hearings before the Subcommittee on Antitrust and Monopoly of the Senate Judiciary Committee on S. 1874. 95th Cong., 1st Sess., 1971, p. 45.

[15] U.S., Congress, House, Congressman Rodino speaking for the Antitrust Improvements Act of 1976, S. 1284, 94th Cong., 2nd Sess., 16 September 1976, Congressional Record 122: 10295.

[16] 431 U.S. 720, 736.

had reported out bills to overrule both Illinois Brick and Hanover Shoe. Neither bill came up for vote before Congress recessed for elections in October of 1978. The National Association of Attorneys General has since made clear its intention to lobby for Congress to reintroduce this legislation when the 96th Congress convenes in 1979.

Overview of the Dissertation

Before beginning an analysis of particular rules and procedures used to enable private parties to enforce the antitrust laws, it would be appropriate to first examine the private enforcement mechanism in more detail. This conclusion seems particularly apt since private enforcement has come under strong attack lately by those who contend that it creates perverse incentives, encourages nuisance suits, and promotes overenforcement of the antitrust laws.[17] Proponents of this view usually recommend that private enforcement be replaced by stronger government enforcement. But public enforcement too, has been strongly criticized for its low penalties and the infrequency with which these penalties are imposed. Chapter II looks at antitrust enforcement as a public good and as such determines the optimal amount of enforcement. This determination is made by developing a general equilibrium model of antitrust enforcement in which the defendant's decisions about whether or not to violate the antitrust laws and the plaintiff's decisions about whether or not to bring suit are simultaneously determined. After the optimal level of enforcement is determined, the relative efficiency of public versus private enforcement is discussed.

---

[17] Kenneth G. Elzinga and William Breit, The Antitrust Penalties: A Study in Law and Economics (New Haven: Yale University Press, 1976).

This chapter concludes that public and private enforcement have positive spillover effects on one another and that the two together are superior to either one alone. Since private enforcement escapes relatively unscathed, it then becomes appropriate to discuss substantive issues raised by <u>Illinois Brick</u>. Specifically, would the <u>Illinois Brick</u> decision or some other rule of standing best satisfy the efficiency and compensation goals of the antitrust laws?

Chapter III asks the question: who bears the burden of the price fixed overcharge? This chapter discusses the incidence of the overcharge under varying conditions of market structure, elasticity of demand, elasticity of substitution between the price fixed good and other inputs, cost conditions and various other factors in the short and long run. Several market pricing models indicate to what extent the incidence of the overcharge falls upon various levels in the chain of manufacturing and distribution or is shifted backwards to other factors of production. The structural conditions of market supply and demand are then examined in a sample of recent price fixing cases brought by the Department of Justice. The important parameters from these cases are applied to the results of the market pricing models just discussed to determine the true empirical incidence of the overcharge burden. These conclusions are important for two distinct reasons. First, compensation of injured parties is itself a legitimate goal of effective antitrust policy. Secondly, to the extent that the party truly injured has a greater incentive to help enforce the antitrust laws by filing suit and seeing it through to completion, it becomes necessary to determine the identity of those truly injured parties.

The fourth chapter demonstrates why the <u>Illinois Brick</u> decision should be overruled by Congress. After reviewing qualitatively all the possible advantages and disadvantages of the <u>Illinois Brick</u> rule, an alternative proposal is offered. The alternative proposal is shown to strictly dominate Illinois Brick in that it preserves all its advantages and does not suffer all of its disadvantages. Then alternate proposals to overrule Illinois Brick are discussed along with the structural and behavioral conditions under which they would be most appropriate. To decide between the available alternative ways to overrule Illinois Brick we must understand the prevailing empirical conditions of market structure, behavior, and legal administration. Chapters V and VI will investigate these empirical questions.

Chapter V, which deals with the administrative costs of enforcement, asks several questions. First, what are the costs to society of the complex proof of passing on and of large multiparty litigation, and what does this imply for the various alternatives to overrule Illinois Brick? Secondly, should we worry about the problem of multiple liability, that is, what are its costs and how prevalent is it? In addition, this chapter discusses recent developments in the enforcement of the antitrust laws by the state attorneys general. Here it is shown that the state antitrust directors, many of whom have drastically increased their antitrust enforcement activities in recent years, may incur considerably fewer costs in enforcing the antitrust laws than do other private plaintiffs.

Chapter VI investigates the final and perhaps most important empirical question of this dissertation. This chapter seeks to determine who sues the price fixer. In particular, it focuses on the direct purchaser to determine to what extent he is an active plaintiff and whether his behavior was changed by the Illinois Brick decision. The identities of those parties (direct or indirect purchasers) who are most willing and able to enforce the antitrust laws are an extremely important factor in determining who should have legal standing to sue antitrust violators.

The final chapter of the dissertation summarizes all the research and makes a policy recommendation for overturning the _Illinois Brick_ decision.

CHAPTER II

ANTITRUST AS A PUBLIC GOOD
PUBLIC OR PRIVATE PROVISION?

The social policy objectives served by the efficient enforcement of the antitrust laws are the deterrence of potential violators and the compensation of victims of antitrust injuries. Such enforcement powers are exercised both by public enforcement agencies and by private plaintiffs injured in their "business or property by reason of anything forbidden by the antitrust laws." While public antitrust enforcement enjoys widespread bipartisan support both by the public and in Congress, and while the private treble damage action has been hailed as the pillar of strong antitrust enforcement by Supreme Court Justices, academics, and corporate plaintiffs and defendants alike, both have come under attack in recent years. This chapter, which will focus primarily on price fixing violations, will reveal and analyze some of the major criticisms of both public and private enforcement. After a framework of analysis is established, the efficiency of public versus private enforcement will be discussed.

The first section of this chapter describes the major sources of discontent with both public and private enforcement of the antitrust laws. The next section explains why antitrust enforcement possesses the qualities of a public good. But the existence of a public good does not imply that it need be publicly provided. Both national and local public goods can be privately supplied, sometimes at lower costs, if the correct incentives are provided. The third section develops a general equilibrium model of antitrust enforcement. In this model the number of antitrust violations and the number of treble damage suits are simultaneously determined by the behavior of plaintiffs and defendants and certain exogenous parameters. Once a definition of efficiency is developed, the exogenous policy parameters are varied in order to achieve "optimal" enforcement. While the model in section three assumes that the antitrust laws are enforced by the private sector alone, the fourth section complicates the analysis slightly by reintroducing the public sector and discussing the spillover or external effects between the public and private sectors. In the fifth section the major arguments of one of the harshest critics of private enforcement are both explained and challenged. The final section establishes relevant criteria with which to judge the relative efficiency of public and private enforcement, and compares the two based on these criteria.

I. Antitrust under Attack

Many writers have emphasized the profitability of violating the antitrust laws.[1] These analyses are based on the profitability of price fixing as compared to the penalties likely to be imposed upon its discovery, discounted by the probability of such discovery. The resulting high benefit/cost ratio of price fixing is due to a multitude of factors some of which are discussed here.

---

[1] See, e.g., Walter B. Erickson, "The Profitability of Violating the Antitrust Laws: Dissolution and Treble Damages in Private Antitrust," 5 Antitrust Law and Economics Review (Summer 1972).

The Department of Justice has at its disposal four different remedies.[2] These remedies are monetary penalties, injunctions, prison sentences, and structural relief, although the latter is not usually relevant for price fixing cases. Prison sentences are rarely imposed, and until recently the maximum fines were miniscule compared to the potential profitability of most price fixing violations. Maximum fines were raised by 1974 legislation to one million dollars for a corporation and one hundred thousand dollars for an individual up from the previous maximum of fifty thousand dollars for both. However, the imposition of maximum statutory penalties is rare. In the most publicized antitrust case ever prosecuted--the electrical equipment conspiracy--the average fine imposed upon each corporate defendant was only $16,550 despite the statutory maximum of $50,000 per count. Although the General Electric Company was convicted of nineteen counts, its total fine was just $437,500, a mere one tenth of one percent of its yearly profit.[3] Not only do the penalties actually imposed fall short of the statutory maximum, but the maximum itself in many instances is considerably less than the potential profitability of price fixing.

Maximum prison sentences were raised from one year to three by the Antitrust Procedures and Penalties Act of 1974. Judges, however, have been extremely reluctant to impose prison sentences for antitrust violations.[4] Although seven company executives received thirty day jail sentences

---

[2]The vast majority of price fixing cases are brought by the DOJ probably because the FTC cannot bring criminal suits. For example, during the 1960-69 period the FTC brought 11 of the 190 total cases filed under the category horizontal conspiracy. See, e.g., Richard Posner, "A Statistical Study of Antitrust Enforcement," 13 Journal of Law and Economics, pp. 365-419.

[3]Elzinga and Breit, p. 56.

[4]It is difficult or even impossible to compare the relative deterrence values of fines and prison sentences without knowing who actually pays

in the Electrical Conspiracy Cases, those who thought that such punishment would signify a new era of antitrust enforcement must have been sorely disappointed. Only 18 cases brought by the government during the period 1966-1973 resulted in the imposition of either jail sentences or probation. In the vast majority of these cases the sentence, if any, was suspended. In only seven cases were prison sentences actually served, representing less than 2% of all government cases commenced during this period.[5] Injunctions, while possibly providing relief to injured victims of antitrust violations, certainly cannot be considered a deterrent. To be an adequate deterrent, expected penalties must be sufficiently greater than the expected profitability of the price fixing to account for the possibility of non-detection. This puts the burden of antitrust enforcement primarily on the shoulders of private plaintiffs in treble damage suits.

Section 4 of the Clayton Antitrust Act, enables private persons injured in their business or property by reason of anything forbidden by the antitrust laws to sue and recover treble damages plus the cost of suit

---

the fines and the precise utility functions of those persons contemplating antitrust violations. The purpose of the present discussion is simply to demonstrate that prison sentences are infrequently imposed. A fuller discussion is contained in Elzinga and Breit, pp. 30-43.

[5] It is difficult to tell whether the incidence of the penalty of incarceration for executives committing antitrust violations has been increasing in recent years. In 1976, only one person was jailed out of a total of 175 persons convicted of antitrust violations. In the next year five violators were sentenced to jail out of a total of 161 convictions. Early in 1978 11 current and former officers of companies manufacturing electrical wiring devices received prison terms of one to three months each. Before concluding that the trend of sentencing is upward two facts should be noted. First, in cases originating in *each* of the years of 1966, 1970 and 1972 in excess of six persons were sentenced to unsuspended jail sentences for antitrust violations. Secondly, the *proportion* of convictions, at least in 1977, remains low. *New York Times*, February 12, 1978, p. F3, and Elzinga and Breit, pp. 34-37.

and reasonable attorney's fees. This provision would seemingly provide windfall recovery for injured plaintiffs therefore providing tremendous incentives to sue and deterrence of potential antitrust violators. Despite the fact that private antitrust suits have outnumbered government suits by more than 15 to 1 in recent years,[6] there are, however, several factors, particularly on the defendant's side, which mitigate the effect of treble damage suits as effective deterrents of antitrust violations. One is §162(g) of the Internal Revenue Code which allows corporate defendants in private suits to deduct as a business expense the full amount of any settlement or judgment provided that the suit was not preceded by a plea of guilty or nolo contendre in a criminal action based on the same facts. One third of the payments are deductable even under such circumstances.[7] Fewer than 25% of all government cases filed during the period 1970-1976 were criminal cases.[8] This provision therefore reduced by approximately one half the expected losses due to the litigation of private claims for a high proportion of violations.

In addition, interest is not paid on treble damages awarded to compensate for the time value of money between the time of violation and the time of recovery.[9] In the case of <u>Hanover Shoe</u> the lag between the original court decision in which United Shoe was convicted of monopolizing,

---

[6] Annual Report of the Administrative Office of the U.S. Courts, 1976, computed from table on page 191.

[7] See generally Antitrust Law Developments, American Bar Association.

[8] Annual Report of the Administrative Office of the U.S. Courts, 1976, computed from table on page 191.

[9] Malcom Wheeler, "Antitrust Treble Damage Actions: Do They Work?", 61 <u>California Law Review</u> 1319 (1973).

and the Supreme Court decision awarding Hanover Shoe treble damages was 14 years. At a modest 10% rate of discount, the present value of one dollar of damage payment was worth only 23¢ at the time of conviction. This alone would effectively reduce the treble damages in real terms to less than single damages. Also juries are thought to reduce their estimates of actual damages or fail to convict when informed that these estimates will be tripled, a phenomenon known as jury nullification.[10] Of all the private antitrust cases that went to judgment on their merits during the period 1965-69 only 20% of the cases favored the plaintiff.[11]

Numerous factors may also mitigate the incentives of plaintiffs to sue for treble damages. Since these factors are more closely related to the substance of the Illinois Brick decision, they are more properly addressed in a later chapter.

While the previous paragraphs may lead some readers to conclude that antitrust is less effective in deterring violators than previously thought, an attack of a wholly different nature was mounted by Kenneth Elzinga and William Breit in their recent book: The Antitrust Penalties: A Study in Law and Economics.[12] Elzinga and Breit contest that rather than being ineffective, treble damage recovery to injured plaintiffs produces overeffective enforcement. They describe three phenomena produced by the incentives inherent in the trebling provision of the Clayton Act which they claim produce massive misallocations and sheer wastage of resources. The first alleged adverse effect of the private treble damage

---

[10] Wheeler, p. 1323.

[11] Posner, p. 383 (computed from table).

[12] Elzinga and Breit, pp. 84-96.

action, the perverse incentives effect, is the tendency of plaintiffs injured by reason of antitrust violations to prolong their injury and increase its magnitude in order to benefit from the apparent windfall of the trebling provision. Why should a potential plaintiff file suit now, when assuming a continuing violation, he can wait till next year and increase his profit? By the same reasoning plaintiffs should want to increase their purchases of the price fixed good if at all possible. Secondly, according to Elzinga and Breit, potential plaintiffs would have incentives to file groundless suits or nuisance suits hoping to get the defendant to agree to a settlement. The third alleged adverse effect of the treble damage action is simply the use of resources in the determination and allocation of damages. One could perhaps extend this line of reasoning further to conclude that overenforcement is produced. Responses to Elzinga and Breit's "Uneasy Case for Treble Damages" will be the substance of a later section. Now we shall turn to a discussion of antitrust policy as a public good.

II. Antitrust--A Public Good

Antitrust enforcement can be considered a public good.[13] The elimination of supracompetitive prices through antitrust policy is a good whose consumers are nonrival and who cannot be excluded from "consuming" its benefits. The establishment of competitive prices for one consumer does not in the slightest way diminish the availability of such competitive prices for any other consumer. (Such a statement should not be confused with the fact that increased demand by subsequent consumers may cause prices to rise when supply is less than perfectly elastic. This is a _competitive_

---

[13]This idea is mentioned in Elzinga and Breit, p. 3, and developed further here.

response, not a contradiction of nonrivalness.) Further, it would be impossible, or at least prohibitively expensive, to exclude a consumer from realizing the benefits of a competitive marketplace. The fact that not all consumers consume those goods whose prices are kept more competitive by virtue of antitrust enforcement should be of no concern to us. Neither is the lighthouse used by all. The important characteristic of a public good is that consumption by one doesn't diminish the quantity available to other consumers; all need not consume in equal quantities.

Sceptics of this public goods classification may contest that predatory or exclusionary practices may be specifically directed toward particular competitors and hence conclude that the elimination of such practices would confer a private benefit, not a public one. But the particular competitors who are aided by the elimination of a predatory or exclusionary practice are no different from the particular consumers who consume goods whose prices were once fixed above the competitive level. The elimination of any anticompetitive practice would serve to improve the economic climate for all consumers and competitors. Lighthouses and public bathing areas are still public goods even though the absence of their provision may injure boatowners and swimmers more than other consumers.

Recent antitrust enforcement by the Department of Justice has to some extent taken the form of prosecuting <u>local</u> price fixing conspiracies such as those in the building materials, bakery products and dairy products industries. The immediate or first order effect of such enforcement has the properties of a local public good, since the beneficial effect of the cessation of supracompetitive prices has as its immediate beneficiaries the residents of the locality in which these industries distribute their product. However, when the Department of Justice prosecutes a local cement price fixing case in Arizona, such an action must have an important deterrent effect on cement producers from all parts of the country, and indeed on all potential price fixers. Thus while the first order effect is concentrated locally (as it was with particular competitors), the potentially more important second order effect, however, the increased deterrence of all potential antitrust violators, is a true national public good. This distinction between these first and second order effect will be crucial in later discussion.

Antitrust policy can be thought of as a more or less efficient public policy response to massive market failure. The market failure to be discussed here--monopoly-like collusive pricing--stems from the inappropriability of the benefits of a competitive market by a single individual or firm in the absence of an institutional mechanism to facilitate private enforcement. Neither can groups of consumers band together to "bribe" a monopolist to cease its anticompetitive pricing, for the transactions costs of such an operation would be prohibitively high (would exceed the "gains from trade").

A public good need not be publicly produced. In many cases the private sector or some appropriate combination of the two sectors can be relied upon to provide a public good with an increase in efficiency. In order to determine the proper mix of enforcement between public and private bodies, it will be necessary to examine more closely the nature of the institutional arrangements of enforcement together with the resulting incentives faced by the public and private sector, the spillover effects between the two sectors, and the comparative efficiency in detection, choice of suits, litigation and imposition of penalties of these two sectors. Before doing so it will be useful to explore the general equilibrium nature of antitrust enforcement. In doing so we can determine the optimal level of provision of this public good--antitrust enforcement.

III. A General Equilibrium Model of Antitrust Enforcement

In order to examine more conceptually the relationships between antitrust enforcement, the deterrence of antitrust violators, and the costs of enforcement, we shall assume the existence of an oversimplified model of the economy containing a large number, N, of equal size firms with risk neutral preferences, no government enforcement, and treble damage provision for recovery. The model attempts to characterize an equilibrium level of antitrust violations and treble damage suits that is simultaneously determined by plaintiff's decisionmaking about bringing treble damage suits and defendant's decisionmaking concerning whether or not to violate the antitrust laws. Decisions of both plaintiffs and defendants are assumed to be a function of probable reactions of each other as well as of exogenous parameters determined mainly by the courts and the legislatures (e.g. standing rules and damage penalties). We shall see that in such an economy, a given set of such exogenous parameters will generally produce an **equil**ibrium value of antitrust violations and number of treble damage suits.

The welfare goal in such an economy should be to minimize the sum of all losses due to undeterred antitrust violations plus the costs of enforcement. Using this general equilibrium framework, we can observe changes in the equilibrium level of violations and of treble damage suits, and thus of total social costs brought about by changes in the exogenous policy parameters. Our goal will be to determine what combinations of exogenous parameters will produce a minimum cost solution. Using this framework, the concept of overenforcement of the antitrust laws can be given meaning. The following paragraphs will describe the plaintiff's side, the defendant's side and the conditions under which the "antitrust violations market" is in equilibrium.

There are N identical firms in our simple economy. There is a single type of antitrust violation possible, price fixing, which is assumed to be profitable to potential defendants and harmful to potential plaintiffs, their customers. There is no need, however, to distinguish between plaintiff's firms and defendant's firms. The two are indistinguishable; indeed the same firm can be both a potential violator and a potential plaintiff for different transactions. Initially class actions are assumed to be impermissible. Such an assumption will be relaxed later to demonstrate the effect of class actions on the efficiency of the solution. Firms injured by antitrust violations will bring suit if and only if the expected gains of such suit exceed their costs. The gains are simply damages (J for Judgment) trebled. Plaintiffs are presumed to have a contingent fee contract with their attorneys equal to a sizable fraction (say 1/3) of trebled damages, $3J$. In addition to these costs plaintiffs are assumed to incur certain costs, L, whether or not the litigation is successful. These costs consist principally of the opportunity cost of the firm's own time incurred in assisting their attorneys with preparing a case.

As we shall see, the effect of these fixed costs is to yield a threshold value of damages below which litigation is uneconomic, with the value of the threshold a function of the likelihood of success in litigation, the size of the fixed costs, and the severity of penalties imposed. An alternative explanation of this same threshold would be the preferences of plaintiffs counsel who are unwilling to undertake a suit for small stakes. Indeed, to the extent that it is the plaintiff's attorneys who solicit their clients to bring treble damage cases, the cost benefit calculus on the part of law firms is equally important in determining the conditions under which treble damage suits are brought. However, since plaintiffs' attorneys are likely to be influenced by the same parameters as are the plaintiffs themselves--the probability of winning, the fixed costs of litigation, and the total damages to be collected--for the purposes of analytical tractability it is useful to assume that the decision-making is done by the plaintiff only.

Plaintiffs face a probability of prevailing on the merits, p, which is exogenously determined by the ease of proving violations and the scope of outstanding violations. p is assumed to be an increasing function of v, the amount (percent) of outstanding antitrust violations. That is, convictions are more likely when antitrust violations become more prevalent. The expected value of a possible suit would then be:

$$E(suit) = p(2J-L) - (1-p)L = 2Jp - L .$$

The expression $2J$ in the first term is treble damages, $3J$, minus the attorney's fee, J. Plaintiffs will sue then if $p > L/2J$. This threshold probability is lower the higher the stakes and the lower the fixed costs of litigation.

The defendants' side is more problematical. They stand to gain by price fixing; yet stand to lose treble damages and pay attorney's fees whether they win or lose, as well as having to pay own costs of defense L, similar to that of the plaintiffs. It is presumed that there are a large proportion of firms who for reason of market structure, demand conditions, basic honesty or other reasons are unwilling or unable to collude to raise prices under any circumstances. However, v percent will violate the antitrust laws depending on the probable expected gains and losses from doing so. Gains are simply J while losses are 3J plus attorney's fees. More accurately, if no suit is brought, expected gains are just (1-s)J , where s is the probability of bringing suit. If, however, a suit is brought, but for some reason the defendant prevails, the net gains are just the benefits from price fixing minus the own and attorneys' costs of litigation. It is assumed here that although defendants do not pay contingency fees as do plaintiffs, their _ex ante_ attorney's bill is the same as plaintiffs, pJ . The net expected gains attributable to winning a suit when there has been a violation is just:

$$s(1-p)(J-pJ-L) .$$

Costs of losing a suit are then:

$$sp(2J+pJ+L)$$

where the 2J is the treble damages _minus_ the gain already accrued.[14] Defendant's net expected gains from price fixing are then:[15]

$$(1-s)J + s(1-p)(J-pJ-L) - sp(2J+pJ+L) = J - 4spJ - sL .$$

Here the first term represents the gains from price fixing which accrue whether or not the defendant is successful. The middle term includes treble damages 3J with probability sp , and attorney's fees pJ with probability s . The last term is simply the own costs of litigation with

---

[14] This formulation has implicitly assumed that the payment of fines is immediate so that no present value calculations complicate the analysis.

[15] The Clayton Act provides that losing defendants pay plaintiffs "the costs of suit, including a reasonable attorney's fee." However, since the statutory fee paid is so small (only a small fraction of the actual fees paid to attorneys), it is ignored in the present analysis.

probability s .

The cutoff probability p below which the defendant will find it profitable to fix prices, is then where $p = [(J - sL)/4sJ]$. This cutoff probability is lower the lower the stakes, the higher the probability of suit, and the higher the own costs of litigation, L . Both individual plaintiffs and individual defendants then face threshold probabilities. Plaintiffs will sue if their perceived probability of winning is sufficiently high and defendants will violate the antitrust laws if their perceived probability of losing a treble damage action is sufficiently low. We shall now show that if plaintiffs' and defendants' perceptions of p , the probability of the plaintiff prevailing, are uniformly distributed about its true value, then the corresponding group behavior will be smooth with sufficiently large N .

The probability, s , that any one potential plaintiff will bring suit against an antitrust violator is:

$$s = s(p,k,L)$$

where k is the multiple of penalties, L is the own cost of litigation, and $s_p > 0$. As the probability, p , of winning rises, so will the likelihood that the plaintiff's expected gains exceed the costs of litigation, thus $s_p > 0$. s times V , the total number of violations, yields the expected total number of suits in the economy, S . Multiplying each side by V we have:

$$S = s(p,k,L) \cdot V$$

If we assume that p , the probability of the plaintiff winning, is an increasing function of the number of outstanding violations, that is $p = p(V)$, $p' > 0$, we have:

$$\frac{\partial S}{\partial V} = s_p \cdot p' \cdot V + s(p,k,L)$$

which is unambiguously positive, since all its terms are positive. Thus:

$$S = S(V,k,L) \quad \text{and} \quad S_V > 0 .$$

On the defendant's side, the probability that he will violate the antitrust laws, v , will be:

$$v = v(p,s,k,L) \quad \text{where} \quad v_p, v_s < 0 .$$

As the probability that a suit being brought against him or that the suit will be successful rises, his likelihood of violation will fall, thus v_p, $v_s < 0$. v times N , the number of firms in the economy, yields the expected total number of antitrust violations, V . Multiplying each side by N we have:

$$V = v(p,s,k,L) \; N .$$

Since p is a function of V and N is a constant we can simplify the function to read:

$$V = V(s,k,L) \quad \text{where} \quad V_s < 0 .$$

Defendants are interested in knowing the probability that a suit will be brought against them, s , given that they violate the antitrust laws. They however, see S ,[16] the number of suits, rather than s , the probability of suit. What is the sign of $\partial V/\partial S$? It is just $(\partial V/\partial s) \cdot (\partial s/\partial S)$ or:

---

[16] This analysis assumes that for sufficiently large N and V , E(vN) and E(sV) approximate V and S respectively.

$$\frac{\partial V}{\partial S} = \frac{\partial V}{\partial \left(\frac{S}{V}\right)} \cdot \frac{\partial \left(\frac{S}{V}\right)}{\partial S} .$$

The first term on the right hand side is just V_s which we know to be negative. The second term reflects the potential violator's expectations as to the meaning of a change in S, that is, the violator's guess as to what has happened to s, the probability of suit, when S, the number of suits, has changed. Let us first assume that the violator has perfect information, that is, he knows the plaintiff's S function. The first term again, $\partial V/\partial(S/V)$ is simply V_s which is negative. The sign of $\partial V/\partial S$ then depends only on the sign of $[\partial(S/V)]/\partial S$, which is totally under the control of the plaintiff. But $[\partial(S/V)]/\partial S$ is just equal to:

$$\frac{V - S\frac{\partial V}{\partial S}}{V^2} .$$

Thus if $V > S(\partial V/\partial S)$ or $V(\partial S/\partial V) > S$ [17] or

$$\frac{\partial S}{\partial V} > \frac{S}{V}$$

then the second term is negative and $\partial V/\partial S$ has the expected negative sign.

This result makes intuitive sense. Violators see S, the total number of suits. To them S is irrelevant, except insofar as they can deduce s, the <u>probability</u> of being sued. If $\partial S/\partial V > S/V$ [$(\partial S/\partial V) \cdot (V/S) > 1$], the marginal propensity to sue exceeds the average

---

[17] This entire term is under the control of the plaintiff, therefore the correct interpretation of $\partial V/\partial S$ is $1/(\partial S/\partial V)$.

propensity to sue (the elasticity of suits with respect to violations exceeds unity), they will know that if S has risen s will also have risen, so they will violate less. The same result is obtained if defendants are ignorant as to the true relationship between $\partial S/\partial V$ and S/V, the marginal and average propensities to sue, provided that they act as if $\partial S/\partial V > S/V$, that is, they use S as a proxy for s. This might happen if defendants do not accurately perceive variations in the number of violations. Assuming now that $\partial S/\partial V > S/V$, we have:

$$S = S(V,k,L) \text{ where } S_V > 0, \text{ and}$$

$$V = V(S,k,L) \text{ where } V_S < 0.$$

Since changing the multiple of penalties k, and the fixed costs of litigation, L, changes the threshold of each plaintiff and defendant, it will change the probabilities of suit and of violations. Thus, $S_k > 0$, $S_L < 0$ and $V_k < 0$, $V_L < 0$.

The antitrust market is in equilibrium when the defendant's view of his likelihood of being sued produces a level of antitrust violations which is consistent with the plaintiff's view. Graphically, equilibrium in the system can be shown quite simply and is shown in Figure 1 below. On the vertical axis is shown the total number of antitrust violations. On the horizontal axis is shown the total number of treble damage suits filed. The defendant's violations are a decreasing function of the number of suits filed; the plaintiff's supply of litigation is an increasing function of the total number of violations. Equilibrium is found when the number of violations and the number of suits are mutually consistent. Both the violation curve and the supply of suits curve assume that the value of the penalty, the cost of litigation, and all other relevant exogenous parameters remain constant.

```
Antitrust
Violations |
          |              S = S(V,k,L)
          |  \         /
          |    \     /
          |      \ /
          |      / \
          |    /     \
          |  /         \
          |             V = V(S,k,L)
          |                   Treble
          |_____Damage
                              Suits
```

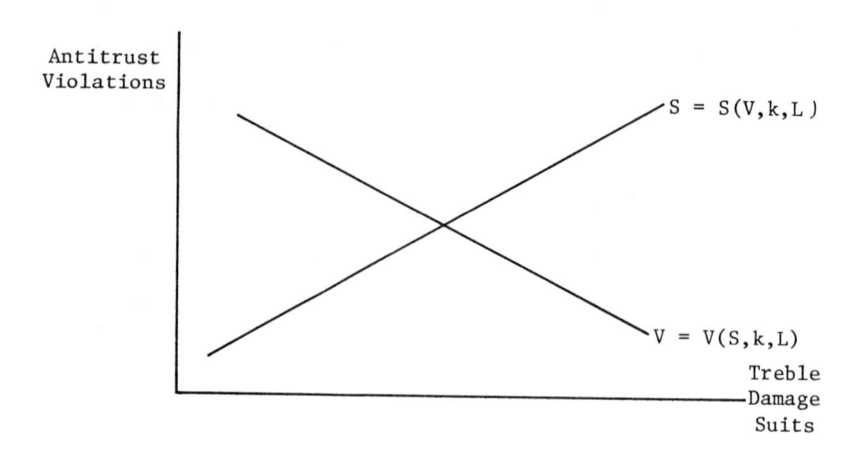

FIGURE 1. The Antitrust Violations Market

How should this antitrust violations equilibrium be characterized? One way would be to observe the costs borne by society in the resulting equilibrium. These losses include both welfare losses due to remaining antitrust violations, and enforcement costs of plaintiffs, defendants, and the courts. The welfare losses are simply the summations of the deadweight losses in each industry plus the internal inefficiency losses resulting from the price fixing. Thus the value of total welfare losses, consistent with our definition of efficiency above, can be read right off the graph in Figure 2. The economic losses due to remaining undeterred violations can be read right off the vertical axis when scaled appropriately to adjust for the cost per violation, and the losses due to the administrative costs of litigation can be read off the horizontal axis, again scaled appropriately to reflect the cost to society of a treble damage suit. More specifically, for a given cost of violation, c^V, and cost of suit, c^S, there is a family of isowelfare cost curves. These will be straight lines with a slope of $-c^S/c^V$. Every point on a given isowelfare cost curve represents some combination of antitrust violations and treble damage suits

```
Violations │
           │ ──────────        S = S(V,k,L)
           │       ──────────
           │ ──────────     ╲ ╱ ──────────
           │       ────────── ╳ ──────────   ⎱ Isowelfare
           │ ──────────     ╱ ╲ ──────────   ⎰ Cost Lines
           │       ──────────
           │ ──────────        V = V(S,k,L)
           │                         Suits
           └──────────────────────────
```

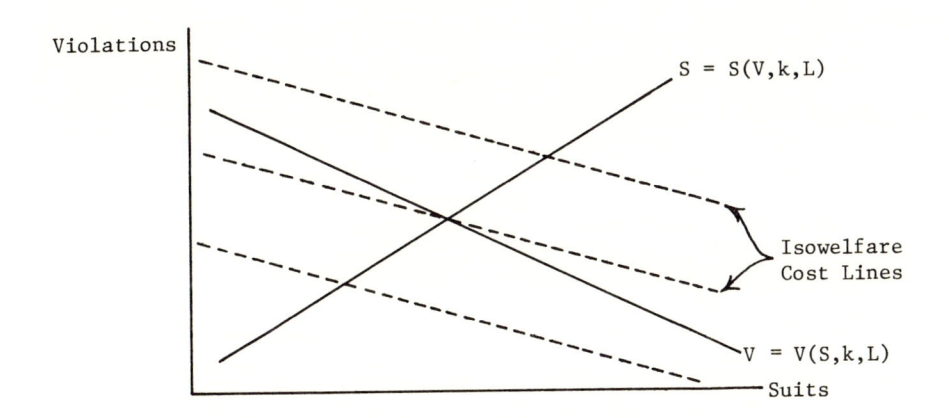

FIGURE 2. A Family of Isowelfare Cost Curves

yielding the same total costs to society. All points to the southwest of a given point are then unambiguously better while points to the northeast are unambiguously worse.

Using this framework we can ask the question of whether antitrust penalties and rewards, and other exogenous parameters, can be altered in such a way to reduce the welfare losses and administrative costs to society of antitrust violations and treble damage suits. We can also ask whether any given exogenous change will reduce the total social costs of violations and treble damage suits. The effects of changes in four exogenous parameters will be shown. First the multiple of penalties will be changed. Secondly, some procedural reforms which result in making antitrust trials simpler and less costly will be assumed. Third, standing rules will be changed to allow more (or fewer) parties to sue. Fourth, class actions will be allowed. Finally, some indication will be given of the qualitative properties of an overall minimum cost solution, where all exogenous variables are permitted to change.

Changes in Penalties

The effect of an increase (or decrease) in the multiple, k, of penalties (and rewards) would be to shift both the defendant's violation curve and the plaintiff's suit curve. Since the defendant's threshold probability of price fixing falls with an increase in penalties, so will the number of violations associated with any given number of treble damage suits. The plaintiff's threshold probability of filing suit also falls as its rewards increase, therefore the number of treble damage suits associated with any given number of violations will rise. The violation curve moves downward and to the left, while the suit curve moves rightward and down. These changes can be seen in Figure 3. The net result produced is fewer violations and more or less suits depending on the slopes of the two curves and the extent to which they shift in response to changes in

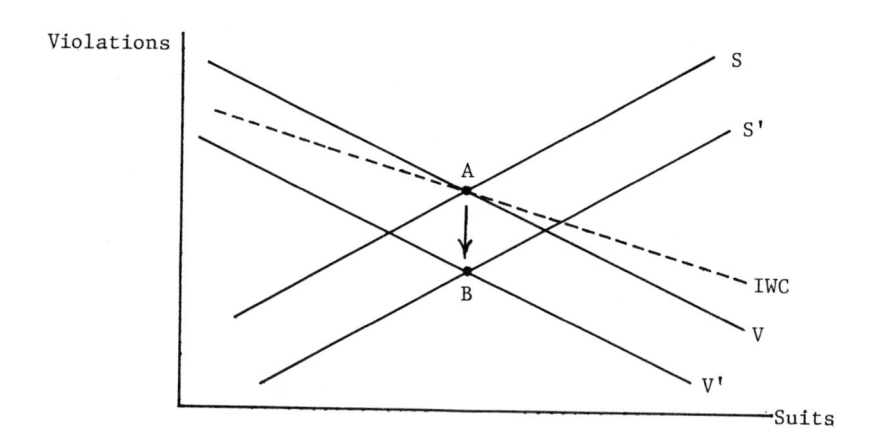

FIGURE 3. The Effect of an Increase in Penalties--a reduction in violations and an unknown change in the number of suits

penalties. If the isowelfare cost line is flatter than the violations curve and it does not move, that is, the cost of suit does not change, we can say unambiguously that we are better off by increasing the multiple of penalties for price fixing.[18] However, the slope may change as penalties are changed. By assuming that the isowelfare cost line moves in response to an exogenous change in penalties, some insights into the nature of an optimal solution can be gained. If the cost to society of a violation is taken to be a given constant, but the social cost of a treble damage action changes in response to a change in penalty levels, the isowelfare cost line will pivot about its intercept on the violation axis. The reason for this might be that as penalties and rewards increase, defendants and plaintiffs would have the requisite incentives to spend more money on their treble damage suits. An increase in the cost of suit would then serve to pivot a given isowelfare cost curve clockwise. Thus, when the costs of suit change in response to a change in penalties, the new equilibrium point must be below the _initial_ isowelfare cost line _after_ it has pivoted in order for society to be better off as a result of the change in penalties. Figure 4 indicates a situation where the increase in penalty makes us better off for we are below our initial isowelfare cost curve. Figure 5 illustrates the opposite. Keeping all other exogenous parameters constant, a welfare maximum will be achieved when we are unable to increase the penalty further without ending up above the initial isowelfare cost line, and we are unable to decrease the penalty without also ending up above the same line after it had pivoted counterclockwise. Moving away from the optimal point would indicate that the marginal gains in one of the endogenous variables, say the marginal gains due to decreased violations, are exceeded by the marginal increases in costs due to more suits and more costly suits.

---

[18] If the isowelfare cost curve _remained_ flatter than the violation curve as penalties continued to increase, the optimal penalty would obviously have to be chosen on grounds other than efficiency.

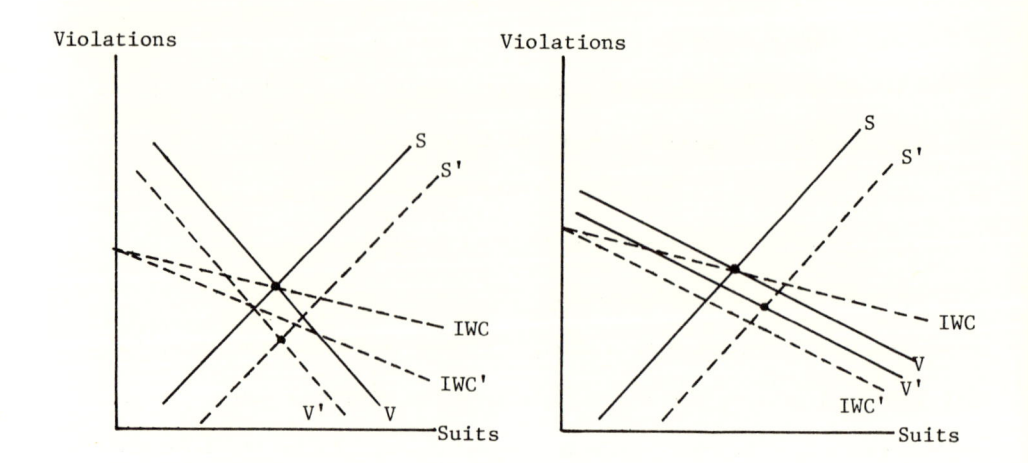

FIGURES 4, 5. The Effect of an Increase in Penalties
when the Costs of Suit May Vary

Change in Costs of Suit

Any procedural or substantive reform which reduces the cost to society of a treble damage suit can be analyzed using the same framework. At first it may seem paradoxical that a reform which serves to decrease the cost of litigation may increase the total social costs of antitrust enforcement. That possibility could occur, though, if the change brought about a large increase in the number of treble damage suits with insufficient compensating reductions in violations.

As a direct result of the reform which reduces the cost of suit,[19]

---

[19] It was assumed above that there are certain fixed costs of litigation, L , which are independent of the value of the suit, and other variable costs which increase with the value of expected damages. Another possible categorization of costs would be exogenous and endogenous costs, that is, costs which the firm has no control over and costs which the firm directly controls. By altering the procedural mechanisms by which firms bring treble damage suits, Federal authorities may control the former costs. Although these two categorizations of costs are very different, changes in exogenous costs are analytically equivalent to changes in L , the fixed costs of litigation and will henceforth be treated that way.

the plaintiff's curve would shift rightward and down since its threshold probability above which it files suit has fallen. The defendant's curve would shift upward and to the right, since its threshold probability below which it fixes prices has risen. Such a change, which can be seen in Figure 6, would produce more suits and an unknown change in the number

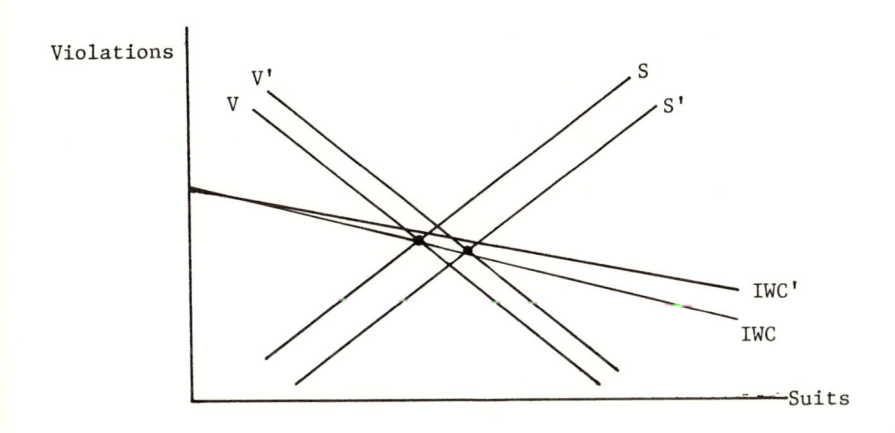

FIGURE 6. The Effect of a Decrease in Costs of Suit

of violations. At the same time, however, the isowelfare cost line has pivoted upward or counterclockwise since the cost of each suit has fallen.[20] An improvement is of course scored when the movement to the new equilibrium point is below the initial isowelfare cost line after it has pivoted upward. An optimum value of exogenously determined costs of litigation would obtain where any movement to a new equilibrium would be above the initial isowelfare cost line. Any further cost reduction from this optimum

---

[20]Plaintiffs and defendants could of course alter their behavior in response to the reform to increase costs elsewhere in the system. Taken to an extreme, endogenous costs could increase sufficiently to fully compensate for the decrease in costs brought about by the government's reforms. In that case, total costs would not decline at all, plaintiff's and defendant's curve would stay put, and the government's reform would then have no effects.

would run into negative returns.

If defendants are assumed to be myopic with respect to the costs of litigation, but plaintiffs take this factor into account in deciding whether or not to bring suit, the conditions under which society would be better off after a reform which decreases the cost of suit can easily be seen.[21] If the defendant is completely myopic with respect to the costs of suit in deciding whether to fix prices, only the plaintiff's curve will shift out. In such a case, the isowelfare cost line being flatter than the violations curve would be a sufficient condition for a welfare improvement. This can be seen in Figure 7. This condition would not be necessary,

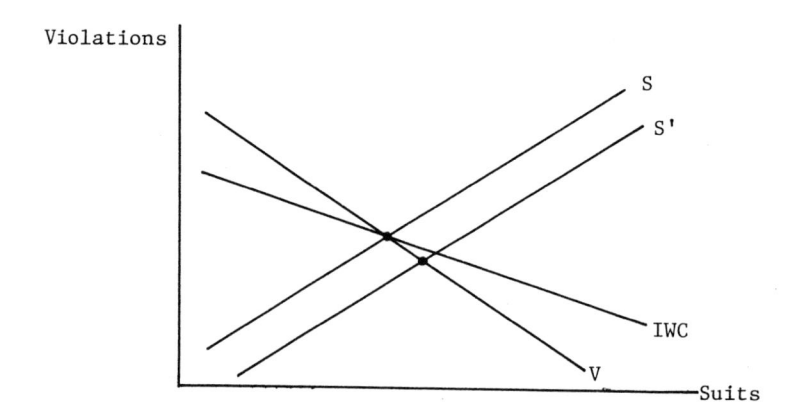

FIGURE 7. The Effect of a Decrease in the Cost of Suit--Defendants are Myopic

---

[21] This assumption is not unreasonable since the defendant's calculations concern whether or not to violate the antitrust laws, whereas the plaintiff's concern whether or not to bring suit. Therefore, the costs of suit are of _immediate_ concern to the plaintiff whereas they may be only secondary to the defendant who may be more concerned with treble damage payments.

however, since this curve will pivot upward as well due to the reduction in the cost of suit. Only if the isowelfare cost line were steeper than the violation curve, and it failed to pivot above the new equilibrium point would we be worse off if the costs of litigation fell. This situation is depicted in Figure 8 below.

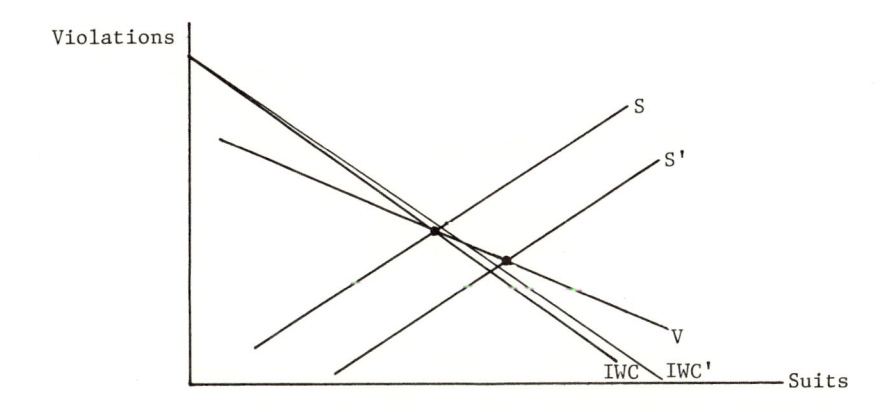

FIGURE 8. The Effect of a Decrease in Cost of Suit--
An Example where Society is Worse Off

Change Standing Requirements

If additional plaintiffs are permitted to sue the price fixer and the average costs of suit do not change in response, the result is quite simple and straightforward and can be seen in Figure 9. The violation curve would remain stationary, as would the family of isowelfare cost curves, by assumption. The plaintiff's suit curve would move to the right and downward by a magnitude which depends on the number of new possible litigants. The result clearly depends only on the relative slopes of the violations and isowelfare cost curves. Therefore, the liberalization of standing requirements, provided that it did not increase the costs per

Violations

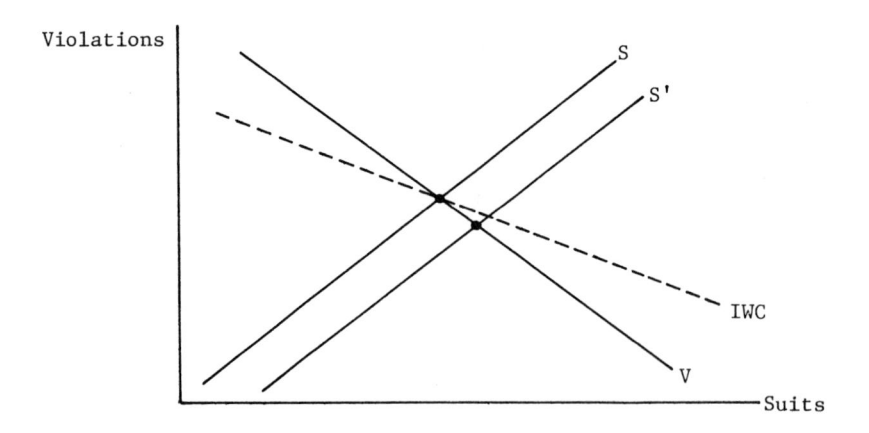

FIGURE 9. The Effect of an Increased Number of Plaintiffs

suit, would be expected to increase overall welfare.[22] This is precisely the <u>Illinois Brick</u> situation.

Class Actions

Up until this point we have assumed class actions to be impermissible. The effect of class action suits on the efficiency of overall enforcement can easily be seen using the general equilibrium framework developed above. Since there are costs of suit which are <u>duplicated</u> by several plaintiffs each bringing separate suits against the same defendant, a consolidation of these separate suits into one single class action would result in a decreased cost of suit <u>per plaintiff</u>. If we switch the label on the horizontal axis of our diagram from the number of suits to the number of plaintiffs suing, the result is easily forthcoming. Since the defendant is deterred by the number of plaintiffs to whom he may have to pay treble

---

[22] It is of course still possible that a liberalization of standing could result in a welfare improvement even though it did serve to increase the average costs of suit. The result would depend, as before, on the position of the new equilibrium point relative to the isowelfare cost line after it had pivoted.

damages, his violations curve remains unchanged.[23] The suit curve moves rightward as treble damage suits become less costly per plaintiff and thus more plaintiffs find it profitable to bring suit. Thus far the situation exactly parallels the one above where standing rules were liberalized. In addition, however, the isowelfare cost line has pivoted upward as the cost per plaintiff has fallen. Therefore, in order for the institution of class actions *not* to be beneficial, the isowelfare cost curve must be steeper than the violations curve *and* pivot so little as not to fall above the new equilibrium point. This situation is especially unlikely when large cost savings are possible with class actions. The normal case is depicted below in Figure 10.

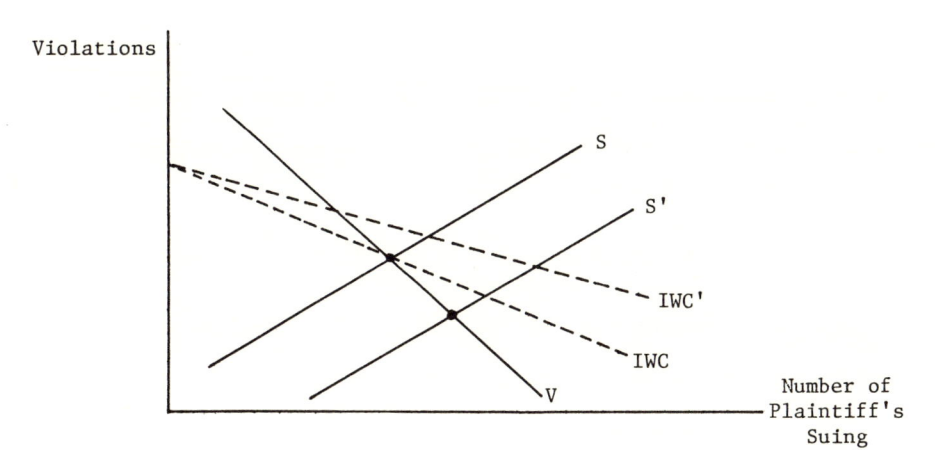

FIGURE 10. The Effect of Class Actions

Thus far we have examined the changes in total costs brought about by a change in a single exogenous variable, such as penalties, while holding all other exogenous variables constant. What would an overall efficient

---

[23] Provided of course that the probability of defendants losing a suit remains constant. This, however, depends only on the number of plaintiffs suing and exogenous parameters, so the curve stays put.

equilibrium look like when all exogenous variables are free to vary? It
certainly is true that all the individual maximizing conditions must hold.
This occurs when any movement away from a given equilibrium due to a change
in a single exogenous variable adds more to costs than it increases benefits. In addition, care must also be taken to assure that we are not
located at a saddle point, that is, a situation where all first partial
derivatives are zero but neither a maximum nor a minimum is achieved.
This is assured only when any movement away from a given equilibrium due
to a change in any combination of exogenous variables adds more to costs
than it adds to benefits.

Having established a framework with which to conceptually measure
efficiency and with which to view the interactions of litigation and violations in a simultaneous model, we turn now to look at the interactions
or spillover effects between public and private enforcement. We begin
first with an examination of the benefits of government enforcement.

IV. The Spillover Effects of Public and Private Enforcement

The economic benefits due to the public enforcement of the antitrust
laws are the restoration of competitive prices in the industry affected
by price fixing and the deterrence of other potential antitrust violators.
In this section it will be shown that since these benefits are exceedingly
small, the principal effect of government enforcement may well be the spillover effects on private parties. To see this we shall first examine the
benefits of public enforcement.

The direct welfare gain of successful government prosecution of
colluding firms in any given industry, ignoring problems of intermediate
goods, is the sum of:

(a) the difference between the consumer surplus gained and the producer surplus lost in the industry--Hargerger's measure of deadweight loss--due to the restoration of competitive prices, plus:

(b) the savings due to the elimination of costs of collusion and internal inefficiencies attributable to such collusion.[24]

To this number should be added:

(c) and (d) the similarly computed gains in those industries <u>deterred</u> from committing antitrust violations by the marginal increase in enforcement in the first industry. This is analogous to a movement up along the violation curve for potential defendants whose probability of violation responds negatively to the outstanding number of suits.

Section 5(a) of the Clayton Act provides that "a final judgment or decree --to the effect that a defendant has violated" the antitrust laws "shall be prima facie evidence against such defendant" in private antitrust actions. Therefore since the government suit may be of substantial benefit to private litigants who later pursue private actions against the same defendant, the <u>information</u> produced by the government is likely to have substantial

---

[24] There are numerous problems with measuring welfare losses by using Harberger triangles. Some are measurement problems, such as the difficulty of measuring the competitive price or the elasticity of demand. Others are conceptual such as the increased welfare losses introduced by vertical distortions. For a general discussion of these issues see F. M. Scherer, <u>Industrial Market Structure and Economic Performance</u> (Chicago: Rand McNally, 1970), pp. 400-411. In addition, the computation of welfare losses through Harberger triangles ignores distributional considerations. It should also be noted that the losses in internal inefficiencies attributable to the higher prices may be considerably larger than the Harberger triangle losses. Since the analysis in the text does not rely on an accurate measurement of losses, but depends more on the concept of welfare losses, these problems are not further addressed.

spillover effects on the private sector's ability to help enforce the antitrust laws. Although there are likely to be no additional benefits in the industry affected, competitive prices already having been restored by the government suit, the increased deterrence of antitrust violators is likely to be greatly strengthened by such spillover. We shall label as (e) and (f) the savings in deadweight losses and internal inefficiency, respectively in the additional industries deterred by the private suits. That (e) and (f) are positive can be seen easily using the analysis of the last section. The addition of private suits for treble damages which piggyback the government suit corresponds simply to an increase in the penalty as seen by the defendant's side, from the government fine to the fine plus treble damages, therefore moving leftward the violation curve of defendants. This unambiguously reduces the outstanding number of violations.

A glance at the available evidence indicates the relative magnitudes of some of these "benefits" of public antitrust enforcement. The deadweight loss is most easily calculable. If, for example, prices are fixed at ten percent above market levels and unitary elasticity of demand is assumed, the deadweight loss is only one half of one percent of sales. If the elimination of these deadweight losses were the sole gains of the Antitrust Division's price fixing enforcement policies, the gains may well fall short of the costs of enforcement! If we take the above measures of elasticity of demand and price markup, minus one and ten percent, respectively, as roughly accurate, and assume that the Division spends half of its time on price fixing, the sales value of the price fixing enjoined yearly would have to exceed $2.5 billion just to justify the yearly budget of the Antitrust Division. When the expenditures of the courts and of private defendants are considered, this number may well increase by an order of magnitude.

To the deadweight losses should be added (b) the relevant magnitudes of savings in internal inefficiency, including the costs of collusion, a quantity difficult to calculate. If the magnitudes of elasticity and percent overcharge used above are again assumed, and <u>all</u> collusive profits are assumed to be dissipated, these losses would be 18 times that of the deadweight loss alone.[25] This assumption, however, is probably highly unrealistic. However, even if the costs of internal inefficiency attributable to the antitrust violation were significant, the sales value of the price fixing enjoined yearly would still have to be quite large to justify the budget of the Antitrust Division.

Most supporters of public antitrust enforcement probably believe that its principal benefits are the deterrence of antitrust violators, that is (c) and (d) above. However, a comparison of the potential gains of price fixing and the fines imposed by the government makes clear the fact that benefits due to the deterrence of antitrust violators must be de minimus. A rational profit maximizing firm is unlikely to be deterred from engaging in a price fixing conspiracy whose value exceeds ten million dollars by the mere <u>possibility</u> of the government's imposition of even its maximum one million dollar fine. The case is even clearer when simply an injunction is involved. Prison sentences remain of minimal deterrence value because of the infrequency of their imposition. As indicated in an earlier section, the cases where prison terms were actually served represent only 2% of all government cases brought by the Department of Justice during the period 1966-73.[26] Therefore, because of the minimal

---

[25] If the competitive price quantity combination is (P,Q) the combination after price fixing would be $(1.1P, .9Q)$. Therefore the rectangle of producer surplus would be $(.1P)(.9Q)$ or $.09PQ$ whereas the Harberger triangle would be only $\frac{1}{2}(.1P)(.1Q)$ or $.005PQ$.

fines imposed by the government when compared to the potential gains from most price fixing violations, and the extremely infrequent imposition of prison sentences, the first order effect of the government action--the welfare increases in the particular industry against which a suit is brought --is likely to be the only substantial effect of such a government suit, absent its effects on the incentives of private plaintiffs to bring their own suits. It is just such minimal deterrence value of government penalties (together with alleged perverse incentive effects of private enforcement to be discussed later) that led Elzinga and Breit to propose a greatly expanded government enforcement program coupled with the elimination of private enforcement.

Given the small deterrence value of the present system of government fines, and the necessarily small magnitude of gains in those industries against which government suits are brought, the greatest benefit provided by government antitrust enforcement may well be the spillover provided to potential private plaintiffs. While a private treble damage action which is based on a previous government suit may produce no direct benefit to society,[27] the secondary effects are likely to be far, far, greater. Welfare increases in other industries produced by the marginal increase in the general level of private enforcement may well be significant, especially since the possible penalty is a sizable multiple of the potential gains from price fixing (as opposed to a small fraction of the potential gains with a government suit). During the early sixties, 85% of all private suits were based on those 20% of government actions where

---

[26] See footnote 4 above.

[27] Since competitive prices should have already been restored by the government suit.

the evidence obtained could be used for a prima facie showing in subsequent private actions based on the same facts.[28] Thus it seems that the information produced by the government in pursuing price fixing violations is itself a true public good. That this information can be later used by private litigants in support of their own private damage actions may well be the most significant benefit from the entire public enforcement program.

V. Breit and Elzinga--The Abolition of Private Antitrust

A number of proposals have recently been made to completely abolish private antitrust enforcement and to replace it with a greatly expanded public enforcement program. The most articulate and complete of such proposals, that of Elzinga and Breit in The Antitrust Penalties, bases its conclusions in part on the perverse incentives faced by private plaintiffs who are injured or potentially injured by violations of the antitrust laws. These authors suggest that since private plaintiffs stand to gain up to three times the total losses sustained by them resulting from a provable antitrust injury, they have every incentive to a) increase the magnitude of antitrust violations affecting them (by purchasing more perhaps), and b) to prolong these violations (or more properly, the injury sustained as a result of these violations). Besides this perverse incentives effect Elzinga and Breit attribute two other harmful effects to the existence of present law and procedure governing private treble damage actions. These are the misinformation effect, the tendency for groundless suits or nuisance suits to be brought by undeserving plaintiffs, and "reparations costs" or the sheer cost of resources used up in the private enforcement of the

---

[28] Posner, p. 372.

antitrust laws.[29]

There appear to be several problems with the reasoning underlying the conclusions of Elzinga and Breit. First, any operation of perverse incentive effects depends crucially on the ability of a buyer to be able to distinguish a price fixing scheme from legitimately higher prices due to higher costs or demand conditions. Their labeling of the private treble damage action as "insurance against poor purchasing"[30] seems to miss this point. Secondly, provided the probability of a successful suit falls short of one, a firm engaging in "perverse" behavior, that is foregoing a current treble damage action so as to increase the payment in the future, gives up _certain_ present income in the form of overcharges on its purchased items in exchange for _uncertain_ future income in the form of treble damages. In an earlier section of their book, Elzinga and Breit discuss the choice of an optimal public policy mix between high enforcement levels and low fines or lower enforcement levels with correspondingly higher fines. In this discussion, they rely heavily on the extreme degree of risk aversity of business firms in order to make their case for the latter solution--very high fines with a relatively lower level of antitrust enforcement.[31] If business firms are as risk averse as Elzinga and Breit would have us believe, they would hardly be anxious to trade certain present losses for uncertain gains especially when the following mitigating circumstances are considered. First, plaintiffs appropriable damages _after_ attorneys fees are paid, are likely to be much closer to double damages than to the

---

[29] Elzinga and Breit, pp. 84-96.

[30] Ibid., p. 89.

[31] Ibid., pp. 120-132.

treble damages that the courts may award. Secondly, if the suit is settled rather than litigated to judgment, a highly probable event, the net value to the plaintiff is likely to be even smaller. Third, interest is never paid on treble damage awards. This factor in conjunction with the first two may reduce the real expected payment to well less than double damages, and may be especially important if the injured firm is liquidity constrained. Additionally if the injured firm engaging in "perverse" behavior competes with other firms who also use the price fixed good, it may sustain considerable short term losses and lose market share should the other firms seek out non-colluding suppliers. And finally, since there is generally a four year statute of limitations for treble damage recovery, if a potential plaintiff uncovers a longstanding violation, postponing suit could have no possible benefit unless the rate of growth of damages exceeded the rate of interest by an amount great enough to compensate for the additional overcharges paid during the years during which litigation is postponed. If the interest rate were 10%, the firm must increase its purchases by a factor of at least 2.21 in order to benefit by postponing suit by a single year.[32] The extension of this four year statute of limitations

---

[32] Assume the firm has sustained damages of magnitude J in each of the last four years. The value of treble damages to this firm is then $12J$. (Assuming for simplicity that damages are paid immediately when the suit is brought, the present value of these damages is also $12J$.) If the firm postpones suit for one year, and in doing so <u>increases</u> its damages to J' in the current year, the present value of its recovery would then be:

$$\frac{9J}{1+i} + \frac{3J'}{1+i} - J'.$$

The break even point would be where:

$$12J = \frac{9J}{1+i} + \frac{3J'}{1+i} - J' \quad \text{or where}$$

$$J\left(12 - \frac{9}{1+i}\right) = J'\left(\frac{3}{1+i} - 1\right).$$

for private antitrust actions applies only in cases where there has been "fraudulent concealment,"[33] which is certainly more difficult to prove, and therefore more risky to try, than the mere existence of compensable antitrust injury.

Any remaining perverse incentives could be ameliorated or even completely eliminated by reform of enforcement policies. The Department of Justice could provide rewards for the quick reporting of those antitrust violations which are eventually prosecuted. In circumstances where a number of plaintifs are injured by the same conspiracy, the plaintiffs would have to collude in order to conceal the injury sustained--for only the first one to report the conspiracy would receive the reward. Also, juries could be instructed to award only double or even single damages where there is evidence that the plaintiff acquiesced in the antitrust violation in order to increase his eventual damage award.[34]

Another potentially serious defect of private antitrust enforcement according to Elzinga and Breit is the potential for groundless suits

---

At an interest rate of 10%

$$J' = \frac{J\left(12 - \frac{9}{1.10}\right)}{\left(\frac{3}{1.1} - 1\right)} = 2.21J.$$

That is J' must exceed J by a factor of at least 2.21 for a plaintiff to find it profitable to delay suit by one year if he were risk neutral. If he were risk averse, as Elzinga and Breit assume elsewhere in their book, J' would have to be even greater. Even if the plaintiff did not discount future treble damage payments, J' would have to exceed J by a factor of 1.5 to make a one year delay profitable.

[33] A pending government suit also automatically tolls the statute of limitations, however, this has no bearing on the present argument.

[34] This could be done while maintaining the trebling provision for damages by depositing the remainder with the U.S. treasury as a penalty. The possibility of creating a wedge between damages and rewards will be considered below in conjunction with the issue of overenforcement.

(harassment suits) to be brought by undeserving plaintiffs who have little to lose and much to gain by the possibility of a large settlement. Harassment suits may originate not only from the plaintiffs themselves, but also from attorneys who may "solicit" potential plaintiffs who appear to have valuable potential claims in treble damages. Elzinga and Breit term this effect the misinformation effect. As considerable resources may be used in the litigation and/or settlement of antitrust claims, a well structured antitrust policy should seek to minimize such suits without, however, discouraging legitimate claims. It can be easily argued that especially where the law is vague, and the outcome of litigation uncertain, an increase in nuisance suits--those based on false claims--would tend to lessen the deterrence value of the antitrust laws. This can be seen quite easily if one imagines the extreme case. If the likelihood of being sued and losing to a plaintiff were the same regardless of whether a violation had actually been committed, then there would be no incentive for the defendant to avoid the violation.

Since the law is relatively clear cut on price fixing, the loss in deterrence value due to infrequent judgments being imposed on innocent defendants should be minimal. Real resources, however, are being consumed in the settlement and litigation process if and when such nuisance suits are brought. Enacting a provision whereby a plaintiff paid the attorney's fees of an innocent defendant in the event that the suit was found to be groundless or utterly without merit would minimize the social losses due to such a misinformation effect, without deterring meritorious claims from being brought. The payment by plaintiffs of defendants attorney's fees in _all_ cases where the plaintiff loses would in general discourage suits, especially by smaller more risk averse plaintiffs and by members of a class.

By limiting the payment of defendant's fees to cases where the suits were totally groundless, legitimate suits would not be discouraged, yet the pure nuisance variety would be. The "gray area"--where the plaintiff loses, but the suit appeared to be meritorious--would be relatively larger where the law is more vague. Such a provision has been enacted into law as part of the <u>parens patriae</u> provisions of the Antitrust Improvements Act of 1976. "--the court may, in its discretion, award a reasonable attorney's fee to a prevailing defendant upon a finding that the State attorney general has acted in bad faith, vexatiously, wantonly, or for oppressive reasons."[35]

The third major alleged fault of private antitrust enforcement is the waste of resources consumed in the enforcement process. Although Elzinga and Breit do not rely on this argument too heavily in making their case for the abolition of private enforcement, we would do well to consider the possibility of <u>overenforcement</u>. At first glance it may appear that a private plaintiff would have an incentive to invest in detection and litigation of antitrust violations in magnitudes which far exceed the societal gain from such investment in enforcement. Indeed, while the deadweight loss is only $\frac{1}{2}(\Delta P)(\Delta Q)$, the potential gains from suit would be $3\Delta PQ$ where (P,Q) is the price fixed equilibrium. Even if all of the gain from price fixing were dissipated in internal inefficiencies and costs of collusion, the trebling provision would keep the potential gains from litigation far greater than the welfare gains to society attributable to antitrust enforcement in that particular industry.[36]

One may be tempted to conclude from this analysis that a rational private plaintiff would face incentives to invest marginal dollars in the

---

[35] §4C(d)(2) of the Clayton Act as amended in 1976.

[36] See footnote 25 above.

enforcement process which produce considerably smaller marginal social gains (although the marginal private gains are of course higher). This analysis of private enforcement ignores the public aspects of private enforcement--the marginal increase in overall deterrence brought about by the increased degree of private enforcement. The question of possible overinvestment in private enforcement, then, hinges on the magnitude of the external effect of the one private damage action on the economy wide welfare losses due to antitrust violations. The trebling provision can be thought of as an incentive necessary to induce the production of this externality or public good.

The correct way to test for overenforcement would be to examine the attainable combinations of violation, suit equilibria to determine if the total social costs inherent in current enforcement efforts exceed the minimal attainable level. Since Elzinga and Breit focus on overenforcement due to excessively high rewards to plaintiffs, the natural response would be to lower those rewards (and thus penalties) to see if the gains or cost savings due to fewer suits exceed the losses incurred due to more violations. This is precisely the problem addressed above.

As indicated in section three above on general equilibrium, overenforcement can only occur if on lowering penalties we end up below the initial isowelfare cost line after it has pivoted upward. As indicated in Figure 11 below, this could occur when the plaintiffs are highly responsive to changes in penalties, but defendants are relatively unresponsive to penalties or to the number of suits. At the same time the plaintiff's and defendant's curves shift, the isowelfare cost line pivots upward to reflect the smaller average cost of suit. Overenforcement would have occurred when the new equilibrium point is below the old isowelfare cost

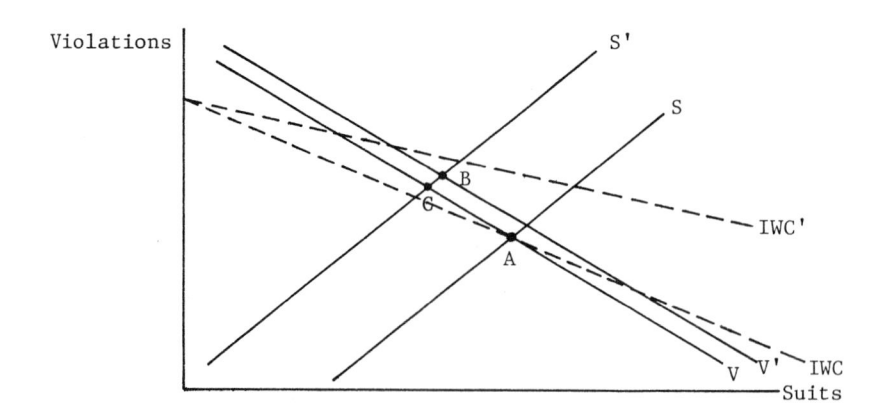

FIGURE 11. An Illustration of Overenforcement

line after it had pivoted upward. The new equilibrium point, B, will undoubtably produce <u>more</u> violations. For overenforcement to have occurred, the reduction in suits or in their costs must be so great as to more than compensate for the cost of an increased number of violations. In the graph above, we have moved from point A to point B.

Although such overenforcement is surely possible, a less drastic means is available to remedy it. The above analysis implied that overenforcement could occur if trebling were more than enough to encourage plaintiffs' suits, the marginal dollars going more to add to the costs of suit than to reductions in violations. On the other hand, the trebling may be necessary to deter defendants. If a wedge were created between penalties and rewards, where defendants were subject to the higher penalties, but where plaintiffs only received a portion of these high penalties as rewards, the equilibrium would move from point B to point C in Figure 11 above. But since we would necessarily be below the new isowelfare cost line IWC' (plaintiff's incentives to spend more money on each suit having been removed) we are unambiguously better off.[37] A wedge between the penalty imposed on the violator and the reward collected by the injured would also serve to further eliminate any perverse incentives effect should they possibly exist.

VI. Public vs. Private--Which is the More Efficient Enforcer?

The argument to this point can be easily summarized. Antitrust enforcement can be considered a public good both because it is nonrival --one person's consumption cannot detract from the amount available to others, and because it is inherently nonexcludable. We have yet to determine though, whether such a public good should be privately or publicly provided. A framework was then developed to depict the relationships between the deterrence of antitrust violators, the scope of outstanding violations and the bringing of antitrust suits by private plaintiffs who are injured in their business or property. This framework focused on the interdependent decisions of potential plaintiffs who must decide whether to bring suit and potential defendants who decide whether to violate the antitrust laws. Together the interaction of defendant's demand for litigation and plaintiff's supply of litigation produce a mutually consistent equilibrium. Efficiency was defined to be the minimization of the welfare costs of undeterred violations and the administrative costs of enforcement. An optimal level of antitrust enforcement has been attained when no changes in exogenous variables can possibly produce another violation, suit equilibrium where the marginal gains exceed the marginal losses.

Both public and private enforcement are subject to severe criticism,

---

[37] This analysis admittedly ignores the fact that defendants may also spend more money defending themselves when the stakes increase. It has also implicitly assumed that the violation curve is steeper than IWC.

yet none are fatal. The principal criticisms of public enforcement focus on its minimal deterrence value due principally to its low penalties. Since penalties could be increased further, these criticisms do not attack the heart of public enforcement. Furthermore, public enforcement was found to lend substantial support to private litigants in pursuing their own damage suits. Similarly with private enforcement, the critics fail to attack the substance of the system. Perverse incentives effects, nuisance suits and overenforcement were found to be considerably less serious than depicted by Elzinga and Breit. Furthermore, even if they are serious, there are less drastic means to remove the perverse incentives without resorting to the extreme solution of abolishing all private suits. This section assumes that the major criticisms of public and private enforcement have been dispelled and proceeds to lay out seven criteria with which to judge the ability of the two sectors to bring cases and to carry them to completion so as to best satisfy the goals of antitrust enforcement. These criteria are: the detection of violators, the availability of resources to proceed with investigation, discovery and trial, economies of scale, incentives to bring important cases, the imposition of penalties, spillover effects, and finally the compensation of injured victims.

Detection

That sector better able to detect antitrust violations would, ceteris paribus, be the more efficient enforcer. The conventional wisdom views the Antitrust Division as a pseudo-passive respondant to complaints received from its daily mail rather than an active player seeking out violations. Such a view is borne out by Hay and Kelly's compilation of the original source of information on recent price fixing cases brought by the Department of Justice. More than a third of the cases were brought to the attention of the Antitrust Division by either customers or competitors of the price fixers, parties who would stand to benefit from bringing a subsequent treble damage suit based on the government suit.[38] Although it is possible that private complaints would still be forthcoming in the absence of private suits, the opposite is not unlikely. Potential plaintiffs have much to gain by complaining should the government obtain evidence which could be later used in their own suit. This incentive to complain to the government would be eliminated if private enforcement were abolished. Providing incentives to complainants might help, but since this policy could be implemented under the current regime, this argument is not compelling for the side of public enforcement. On the other hand, the government regularly uncovers antitrust violations in the process of investigating other cases, particularly in grand jury investigations, a source accounting for almost 25% of all sources of information on cases.[39] The private sector would obviously not have access to this vital source of information.

Considering together all sources of information on detection of price-fixing violations, it appears that the public and private sectors combined are far more able to detect antitrust violations and make them known than are either sector alone. This should not be surprising for the product in question--information--is likely to have public goods qualities and therefore be underprovided by a market system without special incentives. Congress was well aware of the importance of these information flows in enacting the Antitrust Improvements Act of 1976: "Whenever

---

[38] If other private parties are added, including State and Local agencies, current or former employees and others, this total becomes about 60%. George Hay and Daniel Kelly, "An Empirical Survey of Price Fixing Conspiracies," Journal of Law and Economics, p. 21.

[39] Ibid.

the Attorney General of the United States has brought an action under the antitrust laws, and he has reason to believe that any State attorney general would be entitled to bring an action under this Act based substantially on the same alleged violation of the antitrust laws, he shall promptly give written notification thereof to such State attorney general."[40] A high score on detection then, is more probable with both public and private enforcement than with either one alone.

Resources for Discovery and Litigation

Private plaintiffs have available to them the same legal weapons as does the government in their attempts to prove a compensable injury. They may require the production of a defendant's documents, compel the answers to interrogatories, and take depositions. The government, however, has the power to issue a Civil Investigative Demand to private parties. Under the Hart-Scott-Rodino Antitrust Improvements Act of 1976, the government's tools for the investigation of antitrust violations were greatly expanded. CIDs can now be issued to investigate <u>possible</u> violations and can be issued to persons not themselves the target of violations, such as customers, suppliers, and competitors.[41] Private plaintiffs do not have "fishing rights" to investigate possible violations. This is probably wise, for such fishing rights in private hands are likely to be used for purposes other than antitrust enforcement and may well lead to business abuses. On this score, public enforcement clearly has the edge.

---

[40] Clayton Act §4F(a) as amended.

[41] See generally, Earl W. Kinter, Joseph P. Griffen, and David B. Goldston, "The Hart-Scott-Rodino Antitrust Improvements Act of 1976: An Analysis," 46 <u>George Washington Law Review</u>, 1 (November 1977).

Economies of Scale

If there are economies of scale in enforcing the antitrust laws, the concentration of such enforcement would be most efficient. Such efficiencies could be of either the static or the dynamic variety. For the first there could be a minimum efficient scale of building a case and settling or litigating it to completion. For the latter there may be a process of learning by doing whereby cumulative experience would lead to more efficient enforcement. As enforcement is produced by plaintiff's attorneys, the law firm not the business firm is the proper unit in which to examine scale. Since the private plaintiff's antitrust bar is highly specialized (i.e. there exist plaintiff's antitrust law firms), and since such firms coexist in many different sizes, it would appear that any economies of scale are exhausted at a rather small scale. This is especially true since there are no significant barriers to expansion of such plaintiff's antitrust law firms. If unrealized economies of scale did exist, then one would probably see wholesale mergers or large expansions of plaintiff's law firms whether or not the price of litigation was being held above the competitive level. Economies of scale in enforcement then, do not seem to favor public or private enforcement of the antitrust laws.

The many independent sources of initiative inherent in the private enforcement of the antitrust laws may increase the innovativeness of overall antitrust enforcement. Various states in recent years have brought treble damage cases which served to further the creative development of the law. In one of the most famous of these, Hawaii v. Standard Oil Co.,[42] the Supreme Court ruled that a state could not bring suit for injury to its general economy because it would duplicate recoveries that consumers

---

[42] 405 U.S. 251 (1972).

or businesses could obtain under §4 of the Clayton Act. A year later California v. Frito Lay[43] was decided. In that case the State of California attempted to sue not on behalf of its general economy as in Hawaii, but on behalf of citizen consumers to recover monetary damages from firms involved in a price fixing conspiracy. The ninth circuit in Frito Lay recognized the potential benefits of a parens patriae approach to remedying consumer injuries but declined to upstage the legislature. At about the same time the state of New Jersey attempted to recover on behalf of its citizens for injuries sustained as a result of a gasoline price fixing case. It too was denied recovery. Yet in 1976 Congress amended the Clayton Act in passing the Hart-Scott-Rodino Antitrust Improvements Act to allow state attorneys general to sue on behalf of the citizens of their states for treble damages. This is precisely what the state of California was seeking in the Frito Lay case. The law included a provision to assure that multiplicative recovery was not possible—the precise problem the court cited in denying recovery to the state of Hawaii. Again the independent sources of initiative inherent in private enforcement may increase the chances for "technical change" in the antitrust enforcement industry.

Incentives to Bring Important Cases

While it is possible to argue that the Antitrust Division strives to bring the most important cases, it does not have the incentives to do so that the private sector does. In a recent book, The Decision to Prosecute,[44] Suzanne Weaver concludes that the motivations of the more than

---

[43] 474 F. 2d 774 (9th Cir. 1973) cert denied 412 U.S. 908 (1973).

[44] Suzanne Weaver, The Decision to Prosecute: Organization and Public Policy in the Antitrust Division (Cambridge: MIT Press, 1977).

four hundred attorneys in the Antitrust Division are guided much more by bringing and winning as many cases as possible than by any broad view of the economic and social benefits of enforcing the antitrust laws. An overwhelming proportion of the younger attorneys at the Division claimed to have joined in order to get some quick trial experience before going into private practice. This prosecutorial ethos results more from the attorneys' perceived demands of the legal world outside rather than any rewards, promotional or otherwise, within the Division. It would be quite coincidental indeed, if the cases chosen by attorneys guided by the desire to bring and win them as quickly as possible were precisely those cases producing maximal welfare benefits to society.

On the other hand, the rewards to private plaintiffs are determined by the value of the treble damages. Therefore, to the extent that the loss to society attributable to an antitrust violation is correlated with treble damages, private plaintiffs have incentives to bring the most important cases. In addition these larger cases are likely to receive more publicity by the national press and therefore to deter more potential violators. Although the incentives to bring important cases and the social value of antitrust cases may have a high correlation, two qualifications must be made. First, to the extent that the private sector depends on evidence obtained by the government's own cases, the economic value to society of its own suits depends crucially on the decisionmaking back at the Department of Justice. Secondly, to the extent that negotiations between members of a potential class consumes resources, the dispersion of customers of price fixers may adversely affect their incentives to sue.

Recent developments in the offices of the state attorneys general have rendered the incentives faced by states much closer to those of private parties. Revolving funds have been set up by the state legislatures of many states. Money collected by the states in enforcing the antitrust laws can then be used to expand the state antitrust enforcement apparatus. Thus states, like other private parties, have incentives to bring cases in approximate proportion to the economic value to society.

The Imposition of Penalties

Elzinga and Breit propose that all private antitrust enforcement be abolished and that increased public enforcement be substituted. They advocate the imposition of much higher fines than are presently imposed on guilty defendants, specifically mandatory fines equal to 25% of the guilty firm's pre-tax profits for every year of the violation. In most cases this penalty would be much smaller than treble damages.[45] Any

---

[45] Assume that overcharges are a net addition to the profitability of a firm. Then for Elzinga and Breit's proposal to be more expensive to a violator:

$$.25(\pi+D) > 3D$$

where π is the level of profits attainable without price fixing and D is the extent of damages. This is equivalent to:

$$\frac{\pi}{D} > 11 .$$

Since $\quad \frac{\pi}{D} = \frac{K}{O} \cdot \frac{\pi}{K} \cdot \frac{O}{D}$

where K = the capital stock and
O = total output, then

$$\frac{\pi}{D} = k \cdot r \cdot 1/d$$

where k is the capital/output ratio,
r is the rate of return on total capital, and
d is the percent of damages in total output.

$\frac{kr}{d} > 11 \quad$ is required for Elzinga and Breit's scheme to be more costly.

criticism of such a proposal should not be made for having chosen a lower fine per se, for public fines could be raised to the level of treble damages. A more important criticism would be that judges and juries may be far more willing to allow the imposition of a judgment large enough to serve as an effective deterrent of antitrust violations when it also compensates an obviously injured party than when the penalty is merely punative. It was shown earlier that maximum penalties have rarely been imposed even though the statutory maximum is often an order of magnitude or more below the value of the damages. For this reason, the private sector may hold an edge on the imposition of penalties large enough to constitute an effective deterrent.

Spillover Effects

Government antitrust suits may confer tremendous spillover benefits on private antitrust litigants, not only for detection but also by facilitating private litigation by both businesses and the state attorneys general. Section 5(a) of the Clayton Act provides that "a final judgment or decree...to the effect that a defendant has violated" the antitrust laws "shall be *prima facie* evidence against such defendant" in subsequent private antitrust actions. The state attorneys general may benefit even more by Section 4F(b) of the newly amended Clayton Act which provides in part "To assist a State attorney general...the Attorney General of the United States shall...make available to him...any investigative files or other materials which are or may be relevant or material to the actual or potential cause of action under this Act." The Department of Justice

---

Unless the capital intensity of the violating firm is extremely high, or overcharges are placed on only a small proportion of total output, this result is unlikely.

is in a position to provide generous support toward the enforcement of the Federal antitrust laws by the state attorneys general. These state attorneys general are treated as private plaintiffs and therefore may sue in their proprietary capacity for treble damages resulting from illegal overcharges (or damages from other antitrust violations). As state purchases can be quite large, the enforcement practices of these parties can be empirically quite important. The state of California *alone* recovered over $44 million over the period 1973-1977 in treble damages.[46] In addition, the states finally won the battle in 1976 to sue as *parens patriae*, that is, on behalf of the various citizens of their states without the cumbersome problems of class action suits. The potential for states' recovery as *parens patriae* may be far larger than merely recovery as purchasers of price fixed products. For example, the state of New Jersey recovered $3 million for itself and another $3 million for its subdivisions in a 1972 gasoline price fixing case. They remained uncompensated though, for $24 million in estimated damages suffered by the public which *would* have been recoverable under *parens patriae*.[47]

Private efforts may also have positive effects on government enforcement. We have seen this most clearly in the case of the detection of antitrust violators. In the case of *In re Gypsum Wallboard*, plaintiffs made the largest recovery ever collected without the assistance of a prior government suit. A settlement was made in this case for $67.6 million.

---

[46] Testimony of Michael Spiegel, Assistant Attorney General of California, U.S., Congress, House, Committee on the Judiciary, *Effective Enforcement of the Antitrust Laws, Hearings before the Subcommittee on Monopolies and Commercial Law of the Committee on the Judiciary on H.R. 8359*. 95th Cong., 1st sess., 1977, p. 125.

[47] Senate Hearings, p. 93.

The United States asserted its own claims for damages only one day before the statute of limitations had run, thus making good use of the hard work of private parties.[48]

Compensation

Whereas the six criteria used above to judge the ability of the public and private sectors to effectively enforce the antitrust laws all come under a broad efficiency heading, antitrust policy is also concerned with compensating the victims of antitrust injury. Private antitrust wins unambiguously on this score. Although substantial sums are often used to pay plaintiffs' attorneys, and large amounts are often dissipated in providing notice and other expenses in class action suits, no compensation would be provided by government suits alone. Although some may object to the apparent overcompensation of the trebling provision, this trebling is likely to contribute to efficient enforcement as it can be viewed as a payment necessary to induce the provision of a public good by the private sector.

In sum, it appears that the private sector is likely to be at least as efficient, and perhaps more efficient in antitrust enforcement as the public sector, particularly if one considers the ability to detect violations, the incentives to bring the best suits and to impose the highest penalties, and the possibility of greater innovativeness. That private suits are at least as efficient as government suits does not mean that antitrust enforcement should be totally privatized. This is true both because of the superior detection ability of both sectors taken together

---

[48] In re Gypsum Cases, 386 F. Supp. 959, 961 (1974).

than either one alone and also because of the substantial spillover effects of public enforcement on the private sector. That reforms of both public and private enforcement are possible, or even sorely needed, is not in dispute here. The purpose here has been to demonstrate the viability and the superiority of the public and private enforcement system working interdependently to either sector working alone. Now that private enforcement has been shown to be a viable complement to public enforcement, rather than an inferior system rife with perverse incentives and wastage of resources, we can proceed to discuss a particular problem in the private enforcement of the antitrust laws--the <u>Illinois Brick</u> decision.

CHAPTER III

PASSING-ON IN THEORY AND FACT--

WHO BEARS THE BURDEN OF THE OVERCHARGE?

The remainder of this dissertation is concerned with the comparative efficiency and equity of the Illinois Brick decision and alternative rules of standing in private antitrust cases where there are chains of manufacturing or distribution. The identity of injured parties is important in determining to what extent any given rule furthers the compensatory (equity) goal of the antitrust laws. However, it may also be important in the determination of an efficient solution, for injured parties are more likely to enforce the antitrust laws, ceteris paribus, than are non-injured parties. The purpose of this chapter, then, is to determine using various market pricing models and assuming plausible economic conditions, who bears the burden of the overcharge of a price fixed good in a chain of manufacturing or distribution. The bulk of this chapter discusses the theory of the incidence of an overcharge as a function of the market structure of the direct purchaser class, the elasticity of demand for the final good, the elasticity of substitution between the price fixed input and substitute inputs, and various cost conditions, both in the short and in the long run. No attempt is made to assess any general equilibrium effects of the price fixed good; all analyses are partial equilibrium in nature. The remainder of the chapter then applies the results obtained to actual parameters found in real world antitrust cases to reach general conclusions about the passing on of overcharges in chains of manufacturing and distribution. The implications of these conclusions for compensation and deterrence will also be discussed.

The discussion of incidence in this chapter assumes that the price fixer sells its overpriced product to a direct purchaser, who in turn sells to an indirect purchaser, who is also the final consumer. This simple chain from price fixer to direct purchaser to indirect purchaser/final consumer facilitates the analysis and exposition, without much loss of generality, and can easily be extended by lengthening the pass through chain.

It should be noted at this point that the price fixed good can be either a) used by the direct purchaser as a material input in its own production process, b) used as a capital good to manufacture other goods, or c) sold in unchanged form where the value added by the direct purchaser "middleman" is primarily transportation or marketing in nature. In most of the analysis which follows it is assumed that the price fixed good is an input into the production of the direct purchaser's own good. A later section relaxes this assumption.

Section I below discusses and defends the appropriateness of using a partial equilibrium analysis to describe the incidence of a price fixing violation. Section II proceeds to investigate the incidence of an overcharge where the price fixed good is purchased by a monopolist direct purchaser, and where the elasticity of substitution between the price fixed input and other factors of production is zero. The third section demonstrates the extent of passing on under the same fixed proportions assumption, except that the direct purchasers are perfectly competitive firms. Section IV discusses the implications of an oligopolistic structure on the passing-on of overcharges using "Cournot" assumptions. The next section also examines passing-on under oligopoly, but makes alternate assumptions about pricing behavior, such as collusion, price leadership and cost plus pricing. The sixth section complicates the analysis by assuming that the elasticity of substitution for the price fixed input is non-zero. Section VII discusses the special case where the price fixed good is not a material input for the direct purchaser, but is either a capital good or a good which changes hands in unchanged form. Up to this point it has been implicitly assumed that all "burdens" not passed on to the consumer are borne by the direct purchaser. Section VIII considers the possibility that the elasticity of input supplies is less than infinite and therefore some of the burden of the overcharge is shifted backward to other factors of production. The ninth section investigates how the incidence of an overcharge burden might be altered by the insertion of another layer of indirect purchaser between the direct purchaser and the final consumer. Section X reveals the real world incidence of overcharge burdens by applying the theoretical results just developed to a sample of recent price fixing cases brought by the Department of Justice and making general conclusions. Section XI draws some general conclusions about the extent to which injured parties would be adequately compensated under an _Illinois_ _Brick_ rule, and also discusses some general differences between the concept of the incidence of injury as viewed by the economist and injury as viewed by the lawyer. The final section explains why the incidence of an overcharge burden would be an important question even if one were not concerned with compensating the victims of antitrust injuries.

I. In Defense of a Partial Equilibrium Framework

At this point the reader may feel that the proper approach to a study of the incidence of an overcharge due to price fixing would be to utilize the similarity of the problem to that of tax incidence, and accordingly to make use of the immense public finance literature using a general equilibrium framework. This framework has long been used in the field of international trade and was first utilized to study tax incidence by Arnold Harberger. The Harberger model divides the economy into two sectors, corporate and non-corporate, and traces the effect of a tax nominally placed on returns to capital in the corporate sector to changes in net returns to both capital and labor in both sectors as well as relative prices of corporate and non-corporate goods.

The crucial characteristic of the Harberger framework that requires the use of a general equilibrium model is that the taxed sector is relatively large relative to the economy as a whole. The taxed sector is large enough that price changes of the taxed good appreciably affect prices of other products through demand substitution effects, and that migrations of labor and capital to equalize their net returns will in turn affect their economy wide rates of return.

This underlying assumption is not satisfied when price fixing takes place in relatively small sectors of the economy. In such cases we can safely assume away important general equilibrium effects on relative prices through consumer substitution effects. It is also unlikely that the consequent reduction of output and/or factor substitution effects will have any appreciable economy wide effect on factor prices. It is true, however, that <u>close substitutes</u> of the direct purchaser's product may experience significant price increases, and that <u>specialized</u> factors of production may also experience significant price changes.[1] But as these sectors are usually small relative to the size of the entire economy, the problem is adequately handled using a partial equilibrium framework.

II. Simple Monopoly Case

In developing a simple model to determine the extent of overcharge of a price fixed good which is transmitted to a final consumer, the overcharge will first be treated like a unit tax on the output of the final good (e.g. t cents per unit). The assumption underlying this treatment is that the elasticity of substitution for the price fixed good is zero; no substitution is possible. The production function is a fixed factor proportions production function, at least with respect to the price fixed input. This formulation allows for a production relation where there is substitutability among the other inputs. For example:

$$Q = \min\left[\frac{X_1}{a}, \frac{X_2^\alpha X_3^\alpha}{b}\right]$$

where X_1 is the price fixed input of which a units are required to produce one unit of output. Cost can then be expressed as $C = C(Q) + t \cdot Q$ where t is the amount of overcharge per unit of output[2] and where the competitive part of the price of X_1 is incorporated into $C(Q)$. All other factors of production are assumed to be elastically supplied; their prices are taken to be constants by the firm.

---

[1] As we shall see, factor prices may go up or down. This last case will be discussed in Section VIII.

[2] This t represents an overcharge of t/a per unit of input with a units of input required to produce each unit of output.

If the inverse demand curve facing the direct purchaser monopolist, the industry demand curve, is given by $P = f(Q)$, the monopolist's profit equation is simply:

(1) $\quad \pi = Qf(Q) - C(Q) - tQ$.

Maximizing this expression by differentiating with respect to Q and setting the result equal to zero we have:

(2) $\quad Qf'(Q) + f(Q) = C'(Q) + t$.

This simply states that marginal revenue equals marginal cost, the profit maximization equilibrium condition for the monopolist. Rearranging (2) we have:

(3) $\quad -\dfrac{f'(Q)Q}{f(Q)} = \dfrac{f(Q) - (C'(Q) + t)}{f(Q)}$.

Remembering that demand elasticity is just the reciprocal of the left hand side of (3), $-[f(Q)/f'(Q)Q]$, we have the familiar result that:

(3') $\quad \dfrac{P - MC}{P} = \dfrac{1}{\eta}$.

By differentiating (2) above, the equilibrium condition, we can determine the change in output price brought about by a change in a non-substitutable input price:

$$(Qf''(Q) + f'(Q) + f'(Q) - C''(Q))dQ = dt$$

$$\frac{dQ}{dt} = \frac{1}{2f'(Q) + Qf''(Q) - C''(Q)} .$$

By the chain rule $dP/dt = dP/dQ \cdot dQ/dt$, therefore,

(4) $$\frac{dP}{dt} = \frac{f'(Q)}{2f'(Q) + Qf''(Q) - C''(Q)} .$$

If demand is linear, (f'' = 0), and the marginal cost curve is constant (C''(Q) = 0), we have the familiar result that a monopolist passes on exactly half of his cost increase. If, however, $f''(Q) > 0$, the demand curve flattens out as quantity increases, and a greater price increase is required than if $f''(Q) = 0$.[3] Thus if $f''(Q) \geq 0$ is assumed, one half is the lower bound for the value of dP/dt, the extent of pass on, for $C''(Q) = 0$.

If a specific form of the class of demand curves where $f''(Q) > 0$ is assumed, the constant elasticity demand curve, it can be shown that $dP/dt > 1$, the price increase exceeds the cost increase which precipitated it. Assume that demand is given by the equation:

$$P = Q^{-1/\eta}$$

where η is the price elasticity of demand and where $\eta > 1$.[4] The profit equation is just:

(5) $$\pi = Q^{(\eta-1)/\eta} - C(Q) - tQ .$$

The equilibrium condition where marginal revenue equals marginal cost is just:

---

[3] There is no danger that a larger value of $f''(Q)$ will cause the denominator to change signs. This is true because $2f'(Q) + Qf''(Q) - C''(Q)$ is the slope of the marginal revenue curve minus the slope of the marginal cost curve. The marginal revenue curve must cut from above, or $2f'(Q) + Qf''(Q) > C''(Q)$ for a profit maximum to be attained.

[4] η must be > 1 for a non-infinite optimal price.

(6) $$\frac{n-1}{n}Q^{-1/n} - C'(Q) - t = 0 .$$

Differentiating (6) with respect to the overcharge, t, we have:

(7) $$\frac{dQ}{dt} = \frac{1}{\left(\frac{n-1}{n}\right)\left(\frac{-1}{n}\right)Q^{(-n-1)/n} - C''(Q)} .$$

Again since $dP/dt = (dP/dQ) \cdot (dQ/dt)$ we have:

(8) $$\frac{dP}{dt} = \frac{-\frac{1}{n}Q^{-(n+1)/n}}{\left(\frac{n-1}{n}\right)\left(\frac{-1}{n}\right)Q^{-(n+1)/n} - C''(Q)} .$$

Therefore if $C''(Q) = 0$, that is, if costs were constant:

(9) $$\frac{dP}{dt} = \frac{n}{n-1} .$$

Thus dP/dt is always greater than unity for a constant elasticity demand function where $n > 1$. If the elasticity of demand remains constant, the profit maximizing monopolist's price increase would exceed the magnitude of the cost increase of the price fixed input. However, since the monopolist's product is likely to have more substitutes at higher prices, the constant elasticity assumption is somewhat unrealistic. Rather, the elasticity is likely to increase as does price, thus dampening the extent of the price increase.

The term $C''(Q)$ represents the first derivative of the marginal cost curve. If it is positive, marginal costs fall as quantity falls in response to a price increase, thus requiring a smaller price increase than otherwise. If on the other hand, marginal costs were falling with quantity, $C''(Q) < 0$, the price increase would be greater than half the cost increase.

Unless the values of $f''(Q)$, $f'(Q)$, and $C''(Q)$ [5] are known, no clear answer can be given to the question of the extent to which a monopolist direct purchaser passes on a cost increase. If, however, we assume that $f''(Q) > 0$ (and that marginal costs are constant), the extent of passing on of an overcharge by a monopolist would be at least one half.

III. Competitive Direct Purchaser Markets

The analysis of the extent of pass on in a perfectly competitive direct purchaser market is equally straightforward. Here, though, there is a qualitative difference between the short run and the long run because of the zero profit equilibrium condition which must be assumed in the case of a perfectly competitive industry with no entry barriers. Whereas above we implicitly assumed that no entry or exit could occur, in a competitive market entry or exit will occur in response to demand or cost changes until the zero profit equilibrium condition is again satisfied. The analysis can very easily be seen by use of the pair of graphs below depicting both firm and industry equilibrium. Before the overcharge is imposed we have

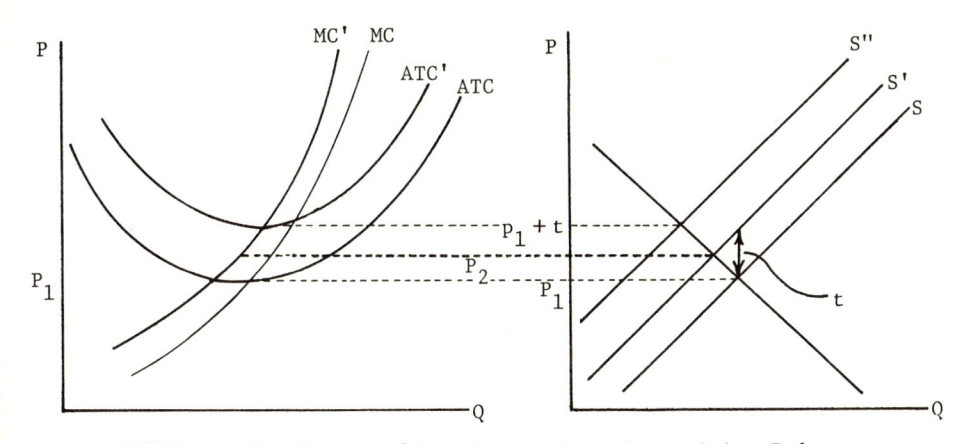

FIGURE 1. The Extent of Passing on in a Competitive Industry

---

[5] Or alternatively the elasticity, in cases where the demand is uniformly elastic in the relevant range.

a firm equilibrium where price equals marginal cost which equals average total cost at its minimum, that is at p_1; and industry equilibrium is found where the quantity demanded equals the quantity supplied--at p_1. The overcharge, amounting to t dollars per unit of production, shifts up the marginal cost curve, the average cost curve and the industry supply curve by \$t. Since demand cannot be completely inelastic, the industry price rises only to p_2 where $p_2 - p_1 < t$; the short run price increase falls short of the overcharge. In the long run, as firms earning negative profits exit the industry, the supply elasticity is effectively infinite and the entire overcharge is passed through.[6] Diagrammatically, the short run industry supply curve has moved leftward to S" as the marginal cost curves of fewer firms are aggregated to produce the total industry supply. Exit will continue until firm profits return to zero; that is, when the price has risen by the amount of the overcharge, t.

Algebraically, if $C = C(q)$ is the cost function of each firm, it becomes $C = C(q) + tq$ after the overcharge is imposed where q is the output of each firm. If all firms are identical, the industry short run supply function can be written as $C'(Q/n) + t$ where $C'(q) + t$ is the marginal cost of each firm. Equilibrium is reached where each firm maximizes profit by setting price equal to marginal cost, and the industry price is set by the market where the quantity demanded equals the quantity supplied. If the (inverse) demand function is $P = f(Q)$, the short run equilibrium occurs where:

(7) $$P = f(Q) = C'\left(\frac{Q}{n}\right) + t .$$

---

[6]This assumes that factor prices and the state of technology are not affected by the size or output of the industry.

To see how changes in t would affect changes in price, differentiate (7) totally to get:

$$f'(Q)dQ = C''\left(\frac{Q}{n}\right)\cdot\frac{1}{n}dQ + dt .$$

Since $dP/dt = dP/dQ \; dQ/dt$, then

(8) $$\frac{dP}{dt} = \frac{f'(Q)}{f'(Q) - C''\left(\frac{Q}{n}\right)\cdot\frac{1}{n}} .$$

What is the <u>ratio</u> of the overcharge passed on to the indirect purchaser to that remaining with the sellers, $(dP/dt)/(1-dP/dt)$? Since the price elasticity of demand, η_D, is just $-(f(Q)/Qf'(Q))$ and the supply elasticity, η_S, is $(f(Q)\cdot n)/(QC''(Q/n))$, the ratio of the overcharge passed on to that remaining with the seller is just:

$$\frac{\frac{dP}{dt}}{1-\frac{dP}{dt}} = \frac{\eta_S}{\eta_D} .$$

As the supply elasticity gets very large (approaches infinity) or as demand becomes more inelastic, the fraction above approaches infinity and 100% if the cost increase is passed on. Thus in a competitive industry, if long run supply is completely elastic, <u>all</u> of the price increase is passed on.[7]

---

[7]This type of analysis cannot be duplicated for a monopolist since a monopolist has no supply curve and thus no well defined supply elasticity.

IV. Oligopoly--Cournot Assumptions

When direct purchasers are neither monopolists nor perfect competitors, but rather oligopolists, we must make certain assumptions as to their pricing policies in order to be able to determine the extent to which they would pass on overcharges due to price fixing. In this section "Cournot" behavior is assumed, whereas in the next section the implications of alternative assumptions are explored. It will be shown that such assumptions do not produce results that are either wildly different from those of monopoly or wholly unexpected. Under plausible sets of conditions the extent of pass on is also intermediate between the two polar cases of monopoly and perfect competition just discussed.

In order to investigate the extent of passing on in such a non-competitive market, assume first a (direct purchaser) industry composed of n identical firms facing an industry (inverse) demand function, $P = f(Q)$. $Q = \sum_{i=1}^{n} q_i$ where Q is total industry output and q_i is firm output. The cost function of each individual firm is $C = C(q_i)$ as before. Again, if the price fixed input has a fixed ratio with output, the individual firm cost function can then be written $C = C(q_i) + tq_i$ where t is the amount of overcharge per unit of final output. The profit equation facing the individual firm is then:

(10) $$\pi = f(Q)q_i - C(q_i) - tq_i .$$

Each firm is a quantity setter, that is, it selects that quantity which yields the highest profits, given the industry demand curve and its own costs. Thus each firm equates marginal revenue and marginal cost assuming that its rivals will not respond to its own moves toward profit maximization. Expression (10) above is maximized by differentiating with respect to q_i and equating to zero to get:[8]

(11) $\quad f(Q) + f'(Q)q_i - (C'(q_i) + t) = 0$.

This is just marginal revenue equals marginal cost. Rearranging terms and substituting Q/n for q_i (since in equilibrium all firms will produce equal amounts) we have:

(11') $\quad \dfrac{f(Q) - C'\left(\dfrac{Q}{n}\right) - t}{f(Q)} = \dfrac{-Qf'(Q)}{nf(Q)}$.

Remembering that price elasticity of demand equals $-f(Q)/Qf'(Q)$ the equation reduces to:

(12) $\quad \dfrac{f(Q) - C'\left(\dfrac{Q}{n}\right) - t}{f(Q)} = \dfrac{1}{n\eta_D}$.

This simply states that the proportional divergence from marginal cost pricing is inversely related to the elasticity of demand. The relevant elasticity, however, is the _firm_ elasticity of demand ($n\eta_d$) rather than that of the industry demand curve, (η_D). In the extreme case where the industry is competitive, the individual firm's demand curve is of course infinitely elastic and price equals marginal cost. In the case of the monopolist we recognize the same result obtained earlier.

To determine how much of an overcharge is passed on to the indirect purchaser, take expression (11) above and differentiate it totally to get:

---

[8] Note that dQ/dq_i is identically equal to one since each firm assumes that its rivals will not react to its own changes.

$$f'(Q)dQ + f'(Q) \cdot \frac{1}{n} \cdot dQ + Qf''(Q) \cdot \frac{1}{n} \cdot dQ = C''\left(\frac{Q}{n}\right) \cdot \frac{1}{n} \cdot dQ + dt \ .^9$$

Finally by rearranging terms and solving for dP/dt which by the chain rule is equal to dP/dQ·dQ/dt :

(14) $$\frac{dP}{dt} = \frac{f'(Q)}{f'(Q)\left[\frac{n+1}{n}\right] + f''(Q)\frac{Q}{n} - C''\left(\frac{Q}{n}\right) \cdot \frac{1}{n}} \ .$$

This is simply the generalized case of the two preceeding ones, competition and monopoly, with an unspecified number of firms and the "Cournot" assumptions. With constant costs, $C''(Q/n) = 0$, and linear demand, $f''(Q) = 0$, the extent of passing on, dP/dt, is n/n+1. As the number of firms grows larger, the pass through approaches unity, the competitive result. As in the case of monopoly if $f'' > 0$, dP/dt is even greater than n/n+1. Also increasing or decreasing marginal costs tend to decrease or increase the price increase that would otherwise have taken place. In general, however, as the number of firms behaving as Cournot oligopolists gets large, the extent of passing on approaches the competitive result: most or all of the cost increase will be passed on, at least in the long run.

V. Oligopoly--Collusion

What happens when firms decide to collude to achieve a joint profit maximizing equilibrium or when firms are not identical but rather there is a dominant firm exhibiting price leadership and numerous fringe firms acting as price takers? Or what happens to an overcharge when firms

---

[9] Note that here $dQ/dq_i = n$ since all firms are identical and do in fact react to changes of its rivals.

implicitly use cost based rules of thumb as coordinating devices for tacit collusion?

The joint profit maximization case is, not surprisingly, almost identical to the monopoly case. If demand and cost functions are $P = f(Q)$ and $C = C(q_i)$ as above and there are n identical firms the joint profit equation is simply:

(15) $$Qf(Q) - nC\left(\frac{Q}{n}\right) + tQ .$$

Therefore the equilibrium condition is just:

$$\frac{\partial \pi}{\partial Q} = Qf'(Q) + f(Q) - C'\left(\frac{Q}{n}\right) + t = 0 .$$

Differentiating this equation yields the same result as with the monopoly, except that the $C''(Q)$ term is replaced by $C''(Q/n) \cdot 1/n$. These two terms are exactly analogous. For a monopolist $C''(Q)$ represents the rate of change of its marginal costs as quantity increases. For the single oligopolist $C''(Q/n)$ is the rate of change of its own marginal costs, therefore since all firms are assumed to be identical, $C''(Q/n) \cdot 1/n$ is the rate of change of industry marginal costs. Thus, except for possible differences in the _value_ of the two marginal cost functions, the result for collusive oligopoly is identical to that of the single firm monopoly.

When all firms are not identical, but rather there is a dominant firm and a competitive fringe the outcome is similar. If the dominant firm is a (short run) profit maximizer and the competitive fringe firms are price takers who equate price and marginal cost, the dominant firm demand curve (DD) can be found by subtracting the competitive supply (CS) horizontally from industry demand (ID). The dominant firm's marginal cost curve (DMC) is assumed to be below that of the competitive fringe.[10] The dominant firm equates its <u>own</u> marginal revenue to its own marginal cost to obtain a maximum value of profits at a quantity of Q_D and a price of P^*. Using this price total industry quantity can be read

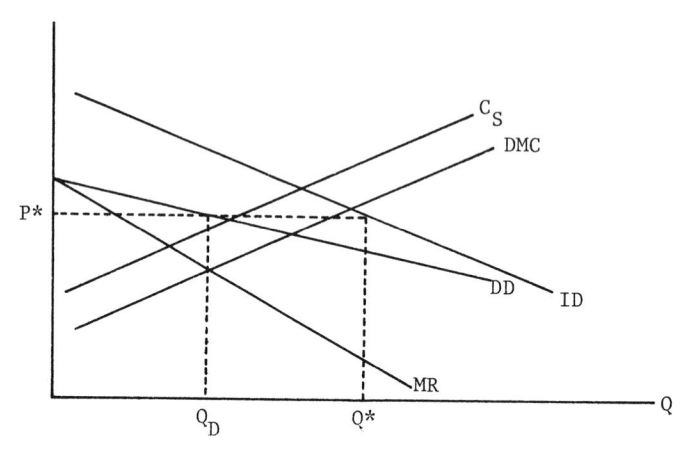

FIGURE 2. Dominant Firm Profit Maximization

off the industry demand curve. The response of the industry to an overcharge which raises the competitive supply curve and the dominant firm's marginal cost curve can be easily shown if we assume linear demand and marginal cost curves. For small cost changes the extent of pass on is directly related to the supply elasticity and inversely related to the demand elasticity. If the two values are equal, the extent of passing on is somewhat greater than one half. As in the case of competitive firms, as the demand elasticity approaches zero and as the supply elasticity approaches infinity, the extent of passing on approaches one. Therefore, unless factor prices change as this industry expands or contracts, the long run supply elasticity should be very elastic and the extent of pass

---

[10] This assumption is not crucial to the result.

on nearly one.[11]

Up until this point in our discussion of Cournot pricing, joint collusive pricing and dominant firm price leadership, we have implicitly assumed that one or more firms have equated marginal revenue to marginal cost in order to achieve a position of profit maximization either for themselves or for the entire industry. There is a large and growing body of literature, however, that indicates that many firms may engage in full cost or cost plus pricing behavior. Such firms are thought to use certain practical rules of thumb such as standard markups, in the setting of prices. A common variant is a markup from average cost at a standard volume of a

---

[11] If the slope of the industry demand curve, dP/dQ, is $-b$, and the slope of both the dominant firm's and the fringe firms' marginal cost curves are β, then after much algebraic manipulation the extent of pass on is shown to be:

$$\frac{dP}{dt} = \frac{3b^2 + 2b\beta}{(\beta+b)(3b+\beta)} .$$

This expression begins to make sense if we differentiate it with respect to b and β. Alternatively we can examine the <u>ratio</u> of the two slopes β and b. Specifically, if $\beta = kb$, then:

$$\frac{dP}{dt} = \frac{3 + 2k}{3 + 4k + k^2} .$$

By differentiating dP/dt with respect to k we get:

$$\frac{-6 - 6k - 2k^2}{(3 + 4k + k^2)^2} .$$

This expression is unambiguously negative. This indicates that as β falls or as b rises, the extent of pass on increases and as β rises or as b falls, the extent of pass on falls.

Since k or β/b is just the ratio of the demand elasticity to the supply elasticity, the extent of pass on is directly related to the value of the supply elasticity and inversely related to the value of the demand elasticity. From the first equation above, if the two values are equal, the extent of passing on is 5/8. Also as k approaches infinity, dP/dt approaches zero, and as k approaches zero, dP/dt approaches one.

large enough magnitude to achieve a target rate of return. Insofar as the magnitude of such markups implicitly takes into account the elasticity of demand, cost plus pricing may approximate short run profit maximization. To the extent that cost plus pricing also takes into account the likelihood of deterring entry, it may also approximate long run profit maximization.

Oligopolistic firms who engage in such markup pricing behavior can be expected to pass on most or all of an overcharge, or in some cases to raise price by an amount greater than their cost increase. These firms who possess some market power and thus recognize their interdependence (though without formally colluding) may use an industry wide cost increase as a ripe opportunity for a price increase. Prices in interdependent oligopolistic industries are often thought to be rigid and price changes infrequent because of the danger that a price increase will go unfollowed and a decrease may break industry discipline. An industry wide cost increase, however, presents an opportune moment for a successful price increase since all firms are likely to recognize both their individual benefit and the likelihood of industry cohesion. To a great extent the common cost increase helps avoid the uncertainty usually present when random price changes occur in interdependent oligopolistic industries. Our maximizing models have universally predicted that most of the cost increase would be passed on. Here as well, the prediction holds. Oligopolists who use standard markup pricing and who adhere to rigid prices due to fears of retaliatory price cutting may well take advantage of such an opportunity to raise prices by an amount equal to or even greater than the cost increase.

Up until this point we have said little about entry except in the case of the competitive industry where entry or exit is assumed to occur until profits return to zero. The conditions of entry are important in determining the extent to which the long run prices established in the marketplace differ from short run prices. In particular, if entry occurs, the long run price will fall.

With a monopoly we implicitly assumed that the barriers to entry were sufficient to preclude entry so that the monopolist's short run price changes correspond with long run price changes. What about oligopoly? If the likelihood or extent of entry is assumed to be proportional to the price cost margin in an industry, then if prices increase by the amount of the overcharge (or less), the likelihood of entry would not be altered (or it would be diminished) by the price increase.[12] Since oligopolists on balance can be expected to conform to this pricing behavior, the likelihood of entry is not altered by the price increase, and short and long run pricing behavior is expected to be similar.

VI. Input Substitutability

Up until this point we have assumed that the direct purchaser cannot substitute away from the price fixed input; his production function is assumed to be one of fixed factor proportions thus requiring a fixed number of inputs per unit of output. Substitution between inputs, at least to some extent, may be possible. Therefore, it would be instructive to consider the implications for the extent of passing on of an overcharge of the producer's ability to substitute away from the price fixed good by using proportionally more of another factor of production.

---

[12] If entry is assumed to be proportional to the rate of return in the industry rather than the price cost margin, the general result is not altered. If constant costs are assumed, a smaller price cost margin will lead to a smaller return on total capital since quantity will have fallen.

Consider a model where a single firm monopolist (the direct purchaser) produces output for final consumption by an indirect purchaser class, using two inputs, one of which is the price fixed good. The production function of the direct purchaser monopolist is described by the equation $Q = f(x_1, x_2)$ where Q is final output and x_1 is the input produced by the price fixing industry. Final demand is described by $Q = g(P)$ where P denotes product price, and the production function is continuous and twice differentiable. Further assume $f_1, f_2, f_{12} > 0$ and $f_{11}, f_{22} < 0$. If both inputs are assumed to be perfectly elastically supplied, the cost to the firm of its inputs is simply $C = p_1 x_1 + p_2 x_2$ where p_i is the price of the ith input. The profit equation of the firm is then:

$$\pi = PQ - C = Pg(P) - p_1 x_1 - p_2 x_2 .$$

By differentiating this profit equation with respect to x_1 and x_2 we obtain the two first order conditions necessary for obtaining a profit maximum. By taking these two equations and the equilibrium condition, indicating that the quantity supplied equals the quantity demanded, we have:

$$Pf_i + \frac{g}{g'} f_i = P_i, \quad i=1,2$$
$$f(x_1, x_2) = g(P)$$

and differentiating all three with respect to the input price p_1, we can then solve a system of simultaneous equations which will give us changes in the three endogenous variables P, x_1 and x_2, given a change in the price fixed input p_1. The change in the product price brought about by a small change in the price fixed input price can be expressed as:

$$\frac{\partial P}{\partial p_1} = \frac{x_1}{2Q} \ .$$ [13]

This simply states that the amount passed on is half the ratio of the price fixed input to output. Thus if an input with a one-to-one ratio with output experiences a price increase of $1, the output price increase will be 50¢. The analogous analysis can be done in the case of perfect competition. With a perfectly competitive direct purchaser market, the extent of pass-on can be expressed as:

$$\frac{\partial P}{\partial p_1} = \frac{x_1}{Q} \ .$$ [14]

Thus even with input substitutability, the extent of pass on of a monopolist direct purchaser is exactly half that of a perfectly competitive industry. The more surprising result though, is that the elasticity of substitution drops out of the expression, that is, the extent of pass on appears to depend only on the number of inputs per unit of output. Does the fact that the elasticity of substitution has dropped out indicate that it is not a determinant of the extent of passing on, $\partial P/\partial p_1$? The answer is clearly no. If the elasticity of substitution were zero, it is clear that the cost of production would increase by the full amount of the overcharge per unit of output. If on the other hand the elasticity of substitution were very large, production costs would not rise by very much and therefore only a very small price increase would be necessary. The

---

[13] The intermediate steps to this result appear in the appendix to this chapter.

[14] See previous footnote.

extent of the price increase depends crucially on the extent to which firms can substitute away from the price fixed input, and this ability depends on the elasticity of substitution. The problem with the analysis above lies only with the inability of the calculus to handle anything but small changes. The following paragraphs explore the effect of the elasticity of substitution on the rate of output price change as one input price changes.

Let us assume that the production function of a direct purchaser firm is described by a CES production function:

$$Q = A[\alpha x_1^{-\rho} + (1-\alpha)x_2^{-\rho}]^{-1/\rho}$$

where $\sigma = 1/1+\rho$. In order to isolate the effect of the elasticity of substitution from other effects such as market structure and pricing policies we shall examine the effect of an input price on the <u>cost</u> of output only. Our problem will be to see how a doubling of one input price is transmitted to the cost of output as the elasticity of substitution varies.

If originally $p_1 = p_2 = \$1$ and p_1 is suddenly raised to $\$2$, what would be the effect on the cost of output after the necessary substitutions have been made? In equilibrium the price ratio of the inputs must equal the ratio of the respective marginal products of these inputs:

$$\frac{p_1}{p_2} = \frac{f_1}{f_2}.$$

Therefore, since

$$f_1 = \frac{\alpha}{A^\rho}\left(\frac{Q}{x_1}\right)^{\rho+1} \quad \text{and} \quad f_2 = \frac{(1-\alpha)}{A^\rho}\left(\frac{Q}{x_2}\right)^{\rho+1}$$

$$\frac{p_1}{p_2} = \frac{f_1}{f_2} = \frac{\alpha}{1-\alpha}\left(\frac{x_2}{x_1}\right)^{\rho+1}$$

$$\frac{p_1}{p_2} = \frac{\alpha}{1-\alpha}\left(\frac{x_2}{x_1}\right)^{1/\sigma}$$

therefore

$$\frac{x_2}{x_1} = \left(\frac{p_1}{p_2}\right)^{\sigma}\left(\frac{1-\alpha}{\alpha}\right)^{\sigma} .$$

This states that the input ratio changes more (from the initial one to one) the greater the input price change, the greater the elasticity of substitution and the smaller α, the factor intensity of x_1. Assume for simplicity that $\alpha = 1-\alpha = 1/2$. Then

$$\frac{x_2}{x_1} = \left(\frac{p_1}{p_2}\right)^{\sigma} .$$

Thus if $\sigma = 0$, the input ratio remains unchanged, whereas it doubles in the Cobb-Douglas case, $\sigma = 1$, and becomes infinite if σ is infinite (x_1 is no longer used at all).

To see how cost changes with the input price change we must substitute the above expression relating the ratio of the two inputs used to their price ratios and the elasticity of substitution back into the CES production function. To simplify the calculation, assume the new input price ratio 2:1 established above. Therefore:

$$Q = \left[\frac{1}{2}x_1^{-\rho} + \frac{1}{2}(2^\sigma x_1)^{-\rho}\right]^{-1/\rho} \quad . \quad 15$$

Since $\sigma = 1/1+\rho$, $-\sigma\rho = \sigma-1$, therefore:

$$Q = \left[x_1^{-\rho}\left(\frac{1}{2} + \frac{2^\sigma}{4}\right)\right]^{-1/\rho}$$

$$Q = x_1\left[\frac{1}{2} + \frac{2^\sigma}{4}\right]^{\sigma/\sigma-1} .$$

Therefore for one unit of Q to be produced x_1 must equal:

$$x_1 = \left[\frac{1}{2} + \frac{2^\sigma}{4}\right]^{\sigma/1-\sigma} .$$

From this equation the absolute and percentage increases in cost resulting from a one dollar increase in the input price can be computed given various values of the elasticity of substitution. The results are indicated in the following table.

---

[15] The constant A has been dropped since it adds nothing to the exposition.

TABLE 1. The Effect of the Elasticity of Substitution on the Cost of Output, $\alpha = 1/2$

σ	x_2/x_1	x_1	x_2	Cost	Percent Passed on*
Before Overcharge	1	1	1	$2.00	--
0	1	1	1	$3.00	100%
.25	1.19	.927	1.100	$2.96	96%
.5	1.41	.854	1.207	$2.91	91%
.8	1.74	.765	1.331	$2.87	87%
1.0	2	.707	1.414	$2.83	83%
1.5	2.83	.569	1.608	$2.75	75%
2.0	4	.444	1.777	$2.67	67%

*Percent passed on is computed as the difference in the cost of output resulting from the overcharge after substitutions are made, divided by the increase in cost which would have occurred if no substitutions had been made. The denominator equals the amount of x_1 originally used or 1 times the one dollar price increase.

It becomes clear on examining the table that the extent of cost increase is not particularly sensitive to the elasticity of substitution when α, the factor intensity parameter, is equal to 1/2.

What happens to the extent of passing on when α is larger or smaller than one half? To see this assume a Cobb-Douglas production function which exhibits a high degree of substitutability between inputs, that is, $\sigma = 1$.

Since in equilibrium the price ratio of the two factors must equal the ratio of their marginal products, we have from above:

$$\frac{x_2}{x_1} = \frac{(1-\alpha)}{\alpha} \left(\frac{p_1}{p_2}\right).$$

Thus initially, before the overcharge is imposed, the amounts of each input used to produce one unit of output at minimum cost are:

$$x_1 = \left(\frac{1-\alpha}{\alpha}\right)^{\alpha-1}$$

$$x_2 = \left(\frac{1-\alpha}{\alpha}\right)^{\alpha}.$$

After the overcharge is imposed $p_1/p_2 = 2$ therefore the input requirements are:

$$x_1 = \left(\frac{2(1-\alpha)}{\alpha}\right)^{\alpha-1}$$

$$x_2 = \left(\frac{2(1-\alpha)}{\alpha}\right)^{\alpha}.$$

Thus both the absolute and percentage change in the cost of producing one unit of output can be seen in the following table for $\alpha = .2$ and $.8$.

TABLE 2. The Effect of the Elasticity of Substitution on the Cost of Output, $\alpha = .2, .8$

		x_2/x_1 (1)	x_1 (2)	x_2 (3)	Cost Before (4)	Cost After (5)	Percent Passed on* (6)
Before		4	.330	1.319	1.649	--	74%
	$\alpha = .2$						
After		8	.189	1.516	--	1.894	--
Before		.25	1.319	.330	1.649	--	92%
	$\alpha = .8$						
After		.5	1.149	.574	--	2.872	--

*The percent passed on is computed as the difference in cost resulting from the overcharge after substitutions are made divided by the increase in cost which would have resulted if no substitutions had been made. Here the denominator is column (2) before the overcharge, times the one dollar cost increase.

If the elasticity of substitution for price fixed inputs is in the same range as for primary factors of production in the American economy, σ has little effect on the cost of output when $\alpha = 1/2$. If the plausible range of σ is taken to be from zero to one, a one dollar input price increase causes the cost of output to rise by a value ranging from $1 to 83¢ at the two extremes. If σ takes a value of one, the input ratio doubles. This is a great deal of substitution! Even when α, the factor intensity parameter, is much greater or less than one half, a relatively large value of σ does not greatly affect the extent of passing on of an overcharge. Therefore, even when some substitutability away from the price fixed input and toward other factors of production is possible, the conclusion that most of the overcharge is passed on to the indirect purchaser is not substantially altered.

VII. Price Fixed Good Not a Material Input

Now that the effects of market structure and the elasticity of substitution have been shown we can safely assume them away in order to isolate the case where the price fixed good is not a material intput but rather is either unchanged by the middleman direct purchaser or a capital good used to manufacture other goods. The middleman case will be handled first. If the direct purchaser is a broker (or wholesaler or retailer), the value added is simply in his marketing of the price fixed good. The analysis is conceptually no different from that above for the price fixed input, except that it is even easier to make a constant costs assumption. Brokers and retailers earning a competitive rate of return will mark up all purchases by their costs and 100% of the overchange is passed on. In West Virginia v. Charles Pfizer,[16] in which part of the antibiotics cases was settled, both wholesalers and retailers indicated that they added a _fixed_ _percentage_ to their cost to determine their price. This means they passed on more than 100% of the overcharge! Although such behavior does not usually characterize a single product competitive industry, most middlemen can be expected to pass on all of an overcharge to the indirect purchaser, at least in the long run.

Where the direct purchaser is a manufacturer using the overpriced good as a capital good in his production process, the result is less straightforward. Where the capital good does not depreciate with the production of output, but only over time, a profit maximizing manufacturer may not raise the price of his product since marginal costs remain unchanged. The price increase would be viewed merely as a fixed cost and may not affect the short run price. In the long run, however, all costs must be accounted for and the price of output will be affected by the overcharged price of the capital good. Where the capital good does depreciate with the production of output, its use is more obviously a marginal cost of production and except if it is not replaced, should affect prices directly. Price fixed goods which take the form of capital goods or remain in unchanged form are no different from raw material inputs for the purposes of determining the extent of passing-on. In the long run most or all of the overcharge is passed on to the direct purchaser.

---

[16] 440 F. 2d 1079 (2d cir. 1971), cert. denied, 404 U.S. 871 (1971).

VIII. Overcharge--A Burden to Other Factors of Production?

Up until this point we have assumed that the burden of the overcharge is either absorbed by the direct purchaser or it is passed on to the indirect purchaser/consumer. There is of course a third possibility; that is, the overcharge could be passed backwards to other factors of production. Before investigating this possibility, it should be mentioned that other factors of production can be affected in two distinct ways. First, their level of employment or quantity used can change, and secondly, their input price can also change. In most of this chapter we have implicitly assumed perfectly elastic input supplies, an assumption which can generate no price changes, only employment changes for substitute inputs. The opposite assumption is made in some general equilibrium models. If input factors are completely inelastically supplied, all changes take place in input prices. In the real world, however, adjustments in demand and cost conditions may have effects on both prices and quantities of inputs, especially when they are "specialized." A completely inelastic supply assumption for substitute inputs would be unrealistic though, because these other inputs used by the direct purchaser are likely to have alternative uses in the economy as a whole and therefore their prices are not likely to be largely affected by their usage by the direct purchaser. The first part of this section will discuss the changes in the quantities used of substitute factors by the direct purchaser. This will enable us to determine, at least qualitatively, whether and to what extent part of the overcharge on a price fixed good may be passed backwards to other factors of production.

It can easily be shown using the framework developed above and elaborated in the appendix to this chapter, that the usage of a substitute factor of production may either increase or decrease when the price of the first factor has increased. The direction of change depends on the relationship between the elasticities of substitution and demand. The magnitude and the direction of change in the use of a substitute factor can most easily be seen using the competitive model above. To approach this question we assume temporarily that factor supplies are perfectly elastic at prices p_1 and p_2. The effect on the usage of x_2 brought about by a change in the price of x_1 can be ascertained using Cramer's rule and the matrix already set up for the analysis of price changes.

$$\frac{\partial x_2}{\partial p_1} = \frac{-g'Pf_{12} - f_1 f_2}{P(f_1^2 f_{22} + f_2^2 f_{11} - 2f_1 f_2 f_{12}) + P^2 g'(f_{11} f_{22} - f_{12}^2)} \quad . \quad 17$$

Since $-g'P$ is equal to elasticity times quantity, and since for a CES production function:

$$f_{12} = \frac{f_1 f_2}{\sigma Q} \quad , \quad f_{11} = \frac{f_1}{\sigma}\left(\frac{f_1}{Q} - \frac{1}{x_1}\right) \quad , \quad f_{22} = \frac{f_2}{\sigma}\left(\frac{f_2}{Q} - \frac{1}{x_2}\right)$$

the numerator reduces to $f_1 f_2 (\eta/\sigma - 1)$ and the denominator to

$$-\left(\frac{f_1}{x_2} + \frac{f_2}{x_1}\right) \cdot \frac{f_1 f_2}{\sigma} \cdot P \quad .$$

Remembering that Euler's Theorem guarantees that $f_1 x_1 + f_2 x_2 = Q$, for functions which are homogeneous of degree one:

$$\frac{\partial x_2}{\partial p_1} = \frac{x_1 x_2}{QP}(\sigma - \eta) \quad \text{where} \quad \eta > 0 \quad .$$

---

[17] See the appendix to this chapter, page 115 for the development of this equation.

Since $f_1 P = p_1$ (marginal physical product times product price equals the input price in equilibrium),

$$\frac{\partial x_2}{\partial p_1} = \frac{f_1}{p_1} \frac{x_1 x_2}{Q}(\sigma-\eta)$$

$$= \frac{x_2}{p_1}\alpha(\sigma-\eta)$$

$$\hat{x}_2 = \hat{P}\alpha(\sigma-\eta)$$

where α is the factor share to $x_1 = f_1 x_1/Q$, and where the symbol ^ denotes a proportional change in the denoted variable. This states that the percentage change in the quantity of x_2 used equals the percent change in the input price times the factor share of x_1, times $(\sigma-\eta)$, the elasticity of substitution minus the elasticity of demand. Therefore if the substitute input is elastically supplied it will gain or lose employment depending on the relationship between the elasticity of substitution and the elasticity of demand.

This very specific result concerning a change in the quantity of x_2 used when it is elastically supplied can be applied at least qualitatively to assess the impact on the price of x_2 of the price fixing of input x_1 after all necessary changes are made. If the elasticity of demand exceeds the elasticity of substitution, then $(\sigma-\eta)$ and $\partial x_2/\partial p_1$ are both negative. The direct purchaser, upon discovering the input price increase, will want to employ less of both factors (while using a higher ratio of x_2 to x_1). The price of x_2 will fall to a greater degree, the greater the discrepancy between the two elasticities, the larger α, the factor intensity parameter, and the greater the input price change. The reverse is also true. If the elasticity of substitution is larger than the elasticity of demand, the firm will attempt to increase its use of the input x_2. This will result in an increase in its price which is larger the greater the difference between the two elasticities, the greater α, and the greater the input price change.[18]

IX. <u>What if the Chain Were Longer?</u>

Up until this point we have discussed the incidence of a price fixed overcharge on two classes of parties in a chain of manufacturing or distribution, the direct and indirect purchasers, under the assumption that the indirect purchaser is also the final consumer. What if the chain were longer? By examining the polar cases of monopoly and perfect competition in an additional indirect purchaser layer, we can ascertain the results of lengthening the chain.

If an additional layer of indirect purchaser were added to the chain of manufacturing or distribution, we then would have a direct purchaser (class), a first indirect purchaser (class), and a second set of indirect purchasers, the consumers. If we confine ourselves to the polar cases of competition and monopoly for the direct and indirect purchaser levels we have four relevant cases: competitive-competitive, competitive-monopoly, monopoly-competitive, and monopoly-monopoly. The analysis of the incidence of an overcharge in all of these cases is straightforward. The addition of an additional layer of competitive firms at the indirect purchaser level will not affect the general result that the consumer bears the brunt of

---

[18] It must be remembered that as the price of x_2 changes in response to changes in the demand for it, this price change will itself influence the extent of substitution from x_1 to x_2.

the overcharge at least in the long run. In the short run each competitive layer would be expected to absorb part of the overcharge depending on demand and supply elasticities. In the long run, however, both sets of competitive firms would pass on all of the overcharge to the final consumers.

When one layer is a monopolist and the other consists of competitive firms, the analysis is very similar to that of the shorter chain where the direct purchaser is a monopolist. Again the addition of competitive firms at any level may serve to absorb part of the overcharge in the short run. In the long run the competitive firms, whether at the direct or indirect purchaser levels, will pass on all of the overcharge. Thus if the single level of monopolist were to absorb less than half of the overcharge, the remainder and major portion would fall upon the final consumer, regardless of the intervening presence of competitive firms.

In instances where both direct and first indirect purchasers are monopolists, the absorption of the overcharge is compounded. Assuming linear demand curves and constant costs, only one fourth of the overcharge is passed on to the final consumer; one half is absorbed by the first monopolist and one half of the remainder by the second. If demand is not linear, but rather $f''(Q) > 0$, then even more of the overcharge is passed on to the final consumer. However, as we shall see in Section X below, the general result that the consumer is most affected by the price fixed overcharge, at least in the long run, remains largely unchanged, since the pure monopoly case is so infrequent.

Up until this point we have implicitly assumed away problems of monopoly power on the buyer's side. For the purposes of analyzing the incidence of an overcharge, there are two interesting monopsony cases;

one where the parties from whom the monopsonist purchases are perfect competitors and one where the party is a monopolist. Where the sellers are competitive firms, the monopsonist will force them to absorb some short run losses by raising its purchase price by less than the amount of the overcharge. In the long run the competitive firms must break even and all charges will be passed on. In the case of bilateral monopoly the result is indeterminate, but rather depends on the relative bargaining strengths of the two parties. In the event that the direct purchaser is a monopsonist his monopsony power may affect the likelihood and extent of the price fixing. In general, however, the lengthening of the chain of distribution to include additional levels of indirect purchasers will not substantially alter the result that especially in the long run, the final consumer will pay for the price fixing.

X. Who Is Injured?--Implications for Compensation

For the purposes of determining the degree to which we achieve success in satisfying the compensation goal under <u>Illinois Brick</u> and various alternative standing rules, it is important to know exactly who is injured in his business or property in "the real world rather than in the economist's hypothetical model."[19] To accomplish this we will first review the theoretical conclusions on the incidence of price fixed overcharges and then apply these conclusions to real world parameters--to a set of recent price fixing cases brought by the Department of Justice.

We have seen that the incidence of an overcharge is dependent on a number of factors such as demand elasticity, input substitutability,

---

[19] Hanover Shoe, 392 U.S. at 493.

cost conditions and market structure. The pass-on was found to be greater with more inelastic demand, more elastic supply conditions, less input substitutability, and more competing firms at the direct purchaser stage. In addition, the extent of passing on is likely to be much greater in the long run than in the short run as cost conditions become more elastic. It will be shown here that when these results are applied to the Antitrust Division's price fixing case load, it appears that in most cases all or nearly all of the overcharge is passed on by the direct purchaser.

The class of cases used here consists of all the price fixing cases brought by the Department of Justice during a recent eighteen month period, January 1, 1977 to July 1, 1978. There are three possible sources of bias in this sample. First, there is not a perfect correspondence between private and government suits. While this is true, the correspondence between them is very high and the non-overlapping suits do not appear to display any peculiar characteristics insofar as the structural conditions of supply and demand are concerned. Secondly, the Justice Department's indictments and civil charges may well be only a small portion of the universe of total violations. Some violations are simply not detected. There is no reason to expect that the incidence of price fixed overcharges is different in detected and non-detected cases. But even more importantly, even if there were important differences, it would be pointless to frame a compensation policy based on the incidence of injury in those classes of cases which are never detected and prosecuted.[20] Third, an indictment does not necessarily imply that a violation has taken place. However, the success rate of the government in getting convictions or guilty or nolo pleas leads

---

[20] It is true, however, that the standing rules chosen might affect the likelihood of detection.

one to conclude that no serious bias is introduced by equating government suits and violations.[21]

The following table lists both civil and criminal cases brought by the antitrust division for price fixing.[22] The first column indicates the Justice Department's bluebook number, and the second column the industry in which price fixing was alleged. The remainder of the columns display the product, the alleged length of time of the conspiracy and the type of buyers (the direct purchaser) when available. In many cases the type of buyer is inferred from rather than explicitly stated in CCH. Bid rigging is included under the category of price fixing, since it is equivalent to price fixing where certain types of services are involved. However, bid rigging directly to the government does not make an interesting observation because, like price fixing at the retail level, there are no indirect purchasers. Therefore, price fixing or bid rigging violations taking place at the retail level only, or directly to the government only were excluded from the sample.

Several observations can be made immediately from a brief glance at the table. First, there is a predominance of price fixing indictments brought against industries such as building materials, paving materials,

---

[21] The sets of government and private cases and violations can be represented by the circles G, P and V respectively. Let X^c represent the complement of set X and let XY represent the intersection of sets X and Y. The first point above reasoned that PG^c and GP^c are small in comparison to PG and furthermore are similar to PG in terms of supply and demand conditions, and thus incidence. The second point argued in part that G is similar to VG^c. The third point argues that V^cG is small.

[22] The information was obtained from Commerce Clearing House, *Trade Regulation Reporter*, Volume 4, New Antitrust Developments.

TABLE 3. Department of Justice Price Fixing Cases

Bluebook Number	Industry	Product	Length of Conspiracy	Buyers
2562	Building materials	Supplies used for drywall, wetwall, swimming pool, ceiling and masonry work	6 years	Construction companies
2564	Bakeries	Sliced white bread	1 year	Grocery stores, restaurants and schools
2565, 66	Cigarettes	Cigarettes	12 years	Retailers
2567	Fresh fruits and vegetables	Transportation of such	8 years	To wholesalers and retailers
2571-72	Portable outdoor toilets	Toilets	Not indicated	To building contractors
2573	Bakery products	Bakery products	7 years	Retailers, governments, school districts
2574	Candy	Candy	2 years	Retailers
2575	Industrial cane sugar	Cane sugar	1 year	To manufacturers of food and beverages
2579-2580	Dairy products	Dairy products	5 years	Retail grocers, restaurants, governments, schools
2587	Anthracite coal	Anthracite coal	13 years	Manufacturers, utilities, distributors

TABLE 3 (continued)

Bluebook Number	Industry	Product	Length of Conspiracy	Buyers
2588	Steel	Reinforcing steel bars	9 years	Construction companies
2591	Armored car service	Armored car service	1 year	?
2597	Furnace pipe fittings	Furnace pipe, ducts, fittings used to install heating and air conditioning in residential and commercial buildings	3 years	Plumbing contractors
2598-99	Furnace pipe fittings	Same as above	3 years	Plumbing contractors
2600-2601	Coatings, resins	(a basic component of paint and other protective and decorative coatings)	3 years	Manufacturers of paint
2602-03	Paving materials	Sand and stone	2 years	Construction companies
2604-05	Paving materials	Ready mix concrete	2 years	Constructions companies
2613-15	Electrical wiring devices	Switches, power outlets	14 years	Electrical contractors
2640	Uranium	Uranium	4 years	Brokers, nuclear reactors, manufacturers
2649	Tires	Replacement tires	6 years	Wholesalers and retailers

102

furnace pipe fittings, electrical wiring devices, and reinforcing steel bars where the goods are sold primarily to construction contractors; and also industrial cane sugar, anthracite coal, and coatings resins where the goods are sold to other manufacturers. In all these cases the price fixed goods comprise a very small or even miniscule proportion of the value of the final product. The derived elasticity of demand for the price fixed good is likely to be very small, and therefore the percentage of pass-on quite high, even in the short run.

Secondly, most of the other products (such as dairy products, bakery goods, and fresh fruits and vegetables) are sold to retailers selling perhaps thousands of goods. These retailers are expected to have very elastic supply conditions and to utilize some sort of cost plus markup pricing system. Therefore they too are expected to have passed on most or all of the overcharge, even in the short run.

Third, although the data in the indictment descriptions are less clear on this point, it appears that the direct purchaser industries are largely competitively structured. We know that when the direct purchaser is a monopolist up to one half of the overcharge may be absorbed rather than passed on, whereas in competitively structured direct purchaser markets, the extent of pass on is likely to be much greater. As most of the industries above are characterized by very inelastic demand conditions, very elastic supply conditions or both, and as few if any direct purchasers are monopolists, the conclusion that even the short run pass on is nearly complete in many industries is borne out empirically.

Lastly, the period during which overcharges of price fixing was alleged by the government is in most cases long enough to constitute the long run. The mean alleged time of price fixing conspiracies in the sample is about 5.5 years, the median 5 years, and at least two thirds are for three years or more. If anything these numbers understate the length of actual price fixing conspiracies since most of the government indictments specify minimum times during which the price fixing conspiracy was alleged to have taken place. The above calculations are those minimum times. In addition, treble damage actions generally follow government actions. Therefore, the conclusion remains that in the vase majority of cases most or all of a price fixed overcharge is passed on by the direct purchaser before treble damage actions are brought.

XI. Implications for Compensation--General

In the last several sections we have argued, both theoretically and empirically, that in the vast majority of cases the bulk of an overcharge due to price fixing is passed on by the direct purchaser even in the short run. The remainder of the burden is felt by the direct purchaser and its non-price fixed factors of production who themselves may experience decreases in factor returns. These results underscore the immense differences between compensation as viewed on the one hand by the antitrust laws in general and by Illinois Brick in particular, and on the other hand by real economic losses as experienced both by firms, individuals, and factors of production. Some of these differences are laid out below.

(1) If Illinois Brick remains law, the direct purchaser (with only a few exceptions) will be the party to collect the damages, whereas it is the indirect purchaser who for the most part bears the burden of the overcharge in the form of a higher price of a purchased final product. For the great majority of cases the party injured will not be the party to collect damages under Illinois Brick, thus the compensatory goal of

the antitrust laws will remain unfulfilled.

(2) This conclusion is generally consistent with the conventional wisdom concerning price fixing. Although there is little or no empirical evidence on this score, most economists believe that price fixing is more likely when demand is inelastic. This is hypothesized from a profitability criterion--the price fixer will lose fewer sales and thus has more to gain from price fixing, ceteris paribus. To the extent that inelastic demand conditions can be equated with the ability of a direct purchaser to pass on an overcharge, price fixing is more likely when indirect purchasers bear relatively more of the burden. This reinforces the conclusion that Illinois Brick is not likely to compensate the injured party.

(3) Even if the indirect purchaser is not badly injured by the overcharge, the direct purchaser may not have absorbed the overcharge, but rather may have passed it back to other (substitute) factors of production. In a competitive industry in the long run all of the overcharge is passed on if long run supply is perfectly elastic. If not the overcharge is divided between factors which are not elastically supplied and consumers. The competitive industry bears no losses in the long run.

(4) In the short run a competitive direct purchaser industry may be substantially injured by an overcharge due to price fixing. There may be a per unit loss before the overcharge can be passed on to consumers or backwards to other factors of production. In addition the volume of sales must necessarily be lower if the price is increased at all. Perhaps even more importantly, firms may have to exit the industry as the increase in price drives buyers to substitute products. The firms which have been most injured--those which have exited the industry--are likely to be unable to collect damages. Those firms who continue to purchase the price fixed

goods and are able to pass on the overcharges, are both least injured and more likely to be able to collect damages.

(5) Similarly with consumers, those who have ceased to consume a product due to its high price are unable to collect damages. Those who continue to purchase the goods, perhaps because their demands are relatively inelastic, are the individuals eligible for damage payment. To the extent that their demands are inelastic, it is ironic that the distortion is least in cases where the collection of damages is most easily available.

(6) Factors of production are never compensated for damages incurred as a result of antitrust violations. Numerous cases dealing with employees and various agents of injured corporations have clearly illustrated this fact.[23] As seen above, substitute factors for the price fixed input can be injured both because their price has fallen and because some may become unemployed. This last statement is not meant to suggest that factors of production *should* be compensated, for the ramifications of an overcharge on prices of products and factors are effectively infinite. It should, however, underscore the vast differences between true economic injury experienced, and the compensatory implications of <u>Illinois Brick</u>. By far the most important difference, however, is that the direct purchaser will collect damages while it is most probably the indirect purchaser who is truly injured.

---

[23] For a detailed exposition of these cases, see Daniel Berger and Roger Bernstein, "An Analytical Framework for Antitrust Standing," 86 <u>Yale Law Journal</u>, April 1977, pp. 820-835.

XII. What If Compensation Were Unimportant?

There is a large and perhaps growing group of economists who believe that the deterrence of antitrust violators is or should be the _only_ legitimate goal of antitrust enforcement.[24] If we were to assume away the value of compensation of injured parties in effective antitrust enforcement and count only the efficiency of enforcement as measured by the sum of welfare losses due to undeterred violations and the costs of enforcement, what would be the significance of the conclusions reached above?

If the sole goal of antitrust enforcement were efficiency, the sole criterion for choosing agents for its enforcement would be their willingness and ability to detect a violation, bring suit and carry it to successful completion at least social cost. To the extent that those injured parties are more willing enforcers, the results obtained above may be as important to the determination of policies to achieve deterrence as they are for compensation. This is particularly true if and when direct purchasers who are not injured by price fixing violations because they have passed on their increased costs and do not want to disturb their relationships with crucial suppliers, do not bring treble damage actions. The importance of this phenomenon will be examined in Chapter 6. The next chapter will begin to examine the alternatives to the _Illinois Brick_ rule.

---

[24] See for example, Richard Posner, _Antitrust Law: An Economic Perspective_ (Chicago: University of Chicago Press, 1976). Also see Robert Bork, _The Antitrust Paradox_ (New York: Basic Books, 1978). Bork argues that efficiency is the only legitimate goal of antitrust enforcement.

APPENDIX TO CHAPTER III

INPUT SUBSTITUTABILITY--MONOPOLY

The monopolist's production function is described by the equation $Q = f(x_1, x_2)$, where Q is final output and x_1 is the input produced by the price fixing industry. Final demand is described by $Q = g(P)$ where P denotes product price, and the production function is continuous and twice differentiable. Further assume that f_1, f_2, $f_{12} > 0$ and f_{11}, $f_{22} < 0$. If both inputs are perfectly elastically supplied, the cost to the firm of its factors is just $C = p_1 x_1 + p_2 x_2$ where p_i is the price of the ith input. The profit equation facing the firm is then:

$$\Pi = PQ - C = Pg(P) - p_1 x_1 - p_2 x_2 .$$

Differentiating with respect to x_1 and x_2 to obtain the first order conditions necessary for a maximum we have:

$$\frac{\partial \Pi}{\partial x_i} = P\frac{\partial Q}{\partial x_i} + g\frac{\partial P}{\partial Q}\cdot\frac{\partial Q}{\partial x_i} - P_i = 0$$

or:

(1) $$Pf_1 + \frac{g}{g'}f_1 = P_1$$

(2) $$Pf_2 + \frac{g}{g'}f_2 = P_2 .$$

Since $P + g/g'$ is equal to marginal revenue, (1) and (2) state that the marginal revenue product of each input equals its price. Further, quantity is a function of price on the demand side and of the amount of each of the two inputs used on the supply side. Therefore, to achieve an equilibrium, the values of p, x_1 and x_2 must produce a consistent value of quantity. More simply the quantity supplied must equal the quantity demanded:

(3) $$f(x_1, x_2) = g(P) .$$

By differentiating the above three equilibrium conditions with respect to the input price p_1, we can then solve a system of simultaneous equations which will give us changes in the three endogenous variables P, x_1 and x_2 given a change in the price of the price fixed input p_1:

$$P\left[f_{11}\frac{\partial x_1}{\partial p_1} + f_{12}\frac{\partial x_2}{\partial p_1}\right] + f_1\frac{\partial P}{\partial p_1} + \frac{g(P)}{g'(P)}\left[f_{11}\frac{\partial x_1}{\partial p_1} + f_{12}\frac{\partial x_2}{\partial p_1}\right]$$

$$+ f_1\left[\frac{g'(P)^2 - g(P)g''(P)}{g'(P)^2}\right]\frac{\partial P}{\partial p_1} = 1 .$$

Rearranging terms we have:

(1') $$f_1\left[\frac{2g'(P)^2 - g(P)g''(P)}{g'(P)^2}\right]\frac{\partial P}{\partial p_1} + f_{11}\left[\frac{g}{g'}+P\right]\frac{\partial x_1}{\partial p_1} + f_{12}\left[\frac{g}{g'}+P\right]\frac{\partial x_2}{\partial p_1} = 1 .$$

Similarly, taking the second equation:

(2') $\quad f_2 \left[\dfrac{2g'(P)^2 - g(P)g''(P)}{g'(P)^2} \right] \dfrac{\partial P}{\partial p_1} + f_{12}\left[\dfrac{g}{g'} + P\right]\dfrac{\partial x_1}{\partial p_1} + f_{22}\left[\dfrac{g}{g'} + P\right]\dfrac{\partial x_2}{\partial p_1} = 0$.

And the third equation:

(3') $\quad g'\dfrac{\partial P}{\partial p_1} - f_1\dfrac{\partial x_1}{\partial p_1} - f_2\dfrac{\partial x_2}{\partial p_1} = 0$.

This gives us three simultaneous equations in three unknowns: $\partial P/\partial p_1$, $\partial x_1/\partial p_1$, and $\partial x_2/\partial p_1$. They can be solved by first arranging them in matrix form and then utilizing Cramer's rule:

$$\begin{bmatrix} f_1 D & f_{11} E & f_{12} E \\ f_2 D & f_{12} E & f_{22} E \\ g' & -f_1 & -f_2 \end{bmatrix} \begin{bmatrix} \dfrac{\partial P}{\partial p_1} \\ \dfrac{\partial x_1}{\partial p_1} \\ \dfrac{\partial x_2}{\partial p_1} \end{bmatrix} = \begin{bmatrix} 1 \\ 0 \\ 0 \end{bmatrix} .$$

Where the following substitutions were made:

D (for demand function term) = $\left[\dfrac{2g'(P)^2 - g(P)g''(P)}{g'(P)^2}\right]$

E (for elasticity term) = $\dfrac{g}{g'} + P$.

It should be noted that if demand is linear, then D will collapse to the value of 2. Further E is simply marginal revenue since marginal revenue = $P + QdP/dQ$. Therefore, by Cramer's rule, the extent of passing on $\partial P/\partial p_1$ will be just:

$$\frac{E(f_1 f_{22} - f_2 f_{12})}{\text{determinant} \begin{vmatrix} f_1 D & f_{11} E & f_{12} E \\ f_2 D & f_{12} E & f_{22} E \\ g' & -f_1 & -f_2 \end{vmatrix}}.$$

where the determinant in the denominator is:

$$E^2 g'(f_{11} f_{22} - f_{12}^2) + DE(f_1^2 f_{22} + f_{11} f_2^2 - 2 f_1 f_2 f_{12})$$

therefore:

$$\frac{\partial P}{\partial P_1} = \frac{f_1 f_{22} - f_2 f_{12}}{E g'(f_{11} f_{22} - f_{12}^2) + D(f_1^2 f_{22} + f_{11} f_2^2 - 2 f_1 f_2 f_{12})}.$$

Similarly, the derived demands for the two inputs x_1 and x_2 are:

$$\frac{\partial x_1}{\partial P_1} = \frac{f_2^2 D + g' f_{22} E}{E^2 g'(f_{11} f_{22} - f_{12}^2) + DE(f_1^2 f_{22} + f_{11} f_2^2 - 2 f_1 f_2 f_{12})}$$

$$\frac{\partial x_2}{\partial P_1} = \frac{-g' f_{12} E - f_1 f_2 D}{E^2 g'(f_{11} f_{22} - f_{12}^2) + DE(f_1^2 f_{22} + f_{11} f_2^2 - 2 f_1 f_2 f_{12})}.$$

To simplify the expression above we shall assume that the demand curve is linear, and make a simple substitution for E. By the first assumption D is equal to 2. Since E is just marginal revenue $P + QdP/dQ$, then $g'E$ is $PdQ/dP + QdP/dQ \cdot dQ/dP = Q + PdQ/dP$ and therefore

$$g'E = Q(1-\eta) \quad \text{where} \quad \eta > 0.$$

We now have:

$$\frac{\partial P}{\partial p_1} = \frac{f_1 f_{22} - f_2 f_{12}}{Q(1-\eta)(f_{11}f_{22} - f_{12}^2) + 2(f_1^2 f_{22} + f_{11}f_2^2 - 2f_1 f_2 f_{12})} \cdot$$

To simplify matters further, assume we are dealing with a CES production function:

$$Q = A[\alpha x_1^{-\rho} + (1-\alpha)x_2^{-\rho}]^{-1/\rho}$$

where $\sigma = 1/1+\rho$ is the (constant) elasticity of substitution. For our purposes it is sufficient to note that all second partial derivatives can be expressed in terms of first partial derivatives:

$$f_{12} = \frac{f_1 f_2}{\sigma Q}, \quad f_{11} = \frac{f_1}{\sigma}\left(\frac{f_1}{Q} - \frac{1}{x_1}\right), \quad \text{and} \quad f_{22} = \frac{f_2}{\sigma}\left(\frac{f_2}{Q} - \frac{1}{x_2}\right).$$

Using these substitutions the numerator of $\partial P/\partial p_1$ easily reduces to:

$$f_1 f_2 \frac{1}{\sigma}\left(\frac{f_2}{Q} - \frac{1}{x_2}\right) - \frac{f_2 f_1 f_2}{\sigma Q} = -\frac{f_1 f_2}{\sigma x_2} \cdot$$

And the denominator is:

$$Q(1-\eta)\left[\frac{f_1 f_2}{\sigma^2}\left(\frac{f_1}{Q} - \frac{1}{x_1}\right)\left(\frac{f_2}{Q} - \frac{1}{x_2}\right) - \frac{f_1^2 f_2^2}{\sigma^2 Q^2}\right] + 2\left[\frac{f_1^2 f_2}{\sigma}\left(\frac{f_2}{Q} - \frac{1}{x_2}\right) + \frac{f_1 f_2^2}{\sigma}\left(\frac{f_1}{Q} - \frac{1}{x_1}\right) - \frac{2f_1^2 f_2^2}{\sigma Q}\right]$$

$$= Q(1-\eta)\left[\frac{f_1 f_2}{\sigma^2}\left(\frac{f_1}{Q} - \frac{1}{x_1}\right)\left(\frac{f_2}{Q} - \frac{1}{x_2}\right) - \frac{f_1^2 f_2^2}{\sigma^2 Q^2}\right] - 2\left[\frac{f_1^2 f_2}{\sigma x_2} + \frac{f_1 f_2^2}{\sigma x_1}\right] \cdot$$

Multiplying numerator and denominator by $\sigma/f_1 f_2$:

$$= \frac{-\frac{1}{x_2}}{Q(1-\eta)\left[\frac{1}{\sigma}\left(\frac{f_1}{Q}-\frac{1}{x_1}\right)\left(\frac{f_2}{Q}-\frac{1}{x_2}\right)-\frac{f_1 f_2}{\sigma Q^2}\right] - 2\left(\frac{f_1}{x_2}+\frac{f_2}{x_1}\right)}$$

$$= \frac{-\frac{1}{x_2}}{Q(1-\eta)\left[-\frac{1}{\sigma}\left(\frac{f_1}{Qx_2}+\frac{f_2}{Qx_1}-\frac{1}{x_1 x_2}\right)\right] - 2\left(\frac{f_1}{x_2}+\frac{f_2}{x_1}\right)}$$

Making use of Euler's theorem for functions which are homogeneous of degree one, $Q = f_1 x_1 + f_2 x_2$, the denominator becomes:

$$Q(1-\eta)\left[-\frac{1}{\sigma}(0)\right] - 2\left(\frac{Q}{x_1 x_2}\right)$$

$$\therefore \frac{\partial P}{\partial p_1} = \frac{-\frac{1}{x_2}}{-2\left(\frac{Q}{x_1 x_2}\right)} = \frac{x_1}{2Q} .$$

This is the result indicated in the text.

Competitive Model with Input Substitutability

Fortunately, the solution of the above problem in a competitive market is a good deal simpler than the problem as posed in a monopoly market. The three equilibrium conditions equivalent to (1)-(3) above are:

$$Pf_1 = p_1$$

$$Pf_2 = p_2$$

$$g(P) = f(x_1, x_2) .$$

The additional simplicity stems from the fact that the input price equals marginal physical product times price, not marginal revenue since the competitive firms are price takers. Differentiating the three equations we get:

$$P\left(f_{11} \frac{\partial x_1}{\partial p_1} + f_{12} \frac{\partial x_2}{\partial p_1}\right) + f_1 \frac{\partial P}{\partial p_1} = 1$$

$$P\left(f_{12} \frac{\partial x_1}{\partial p_1} + f_{22} \frac{\partial x_2}{\partial p_1}\right) + f_2 \frac{\partial P}{\partial p_1} = 0$$

$$g'\left(\frac{\partial P}{\partial p_1}\right) - f_1 \frac{\partial x_1}{\partial p_1} - f_2 \frac{\partial x_2}{\partial p_1} = 0.$$

In matrix form these equations become:

$$\begin{bmatrix} f_1 & Pf_{11} & Pf_{12} \\ f_2 & Pf_{12} & Pf_{22} \\ g' & -f_1 & -f_2 \end{bmatrix} \begin{bmatrix} \frac{\partial P}{\partial p_1} \\ \frac{\partial x_1}{\partial p_1} \\ \frac{\partial x_2}{\partial p_1} \end{bmatrix} = \begin{bmatrix} 1 \\ 0 \\ 0 \end{bmatrix}$$

Solving for $\partial P/\partial p_1$ by using Cramer's rule again gives us:

$$\frac{\partial P}{\partial p_1} = \frac{P(f_1 f_{22} - f_2 f_{12})}{P(-f_1 f_2 f_{12} - f_1 f_2 f_{12} + f_1^2 f_{22} + f_2^2 f_{11}) + P^2 g'(f_{11} f_{22} - f_{12}^2)}$$

$$= \frac{f_1 f_{22} - f_2 f_{12}}{(f_1^2 f_{22} + f_2^2 f_{11} - 2 f_1 f_2 f_{12}) + Pg'(f_{11} f_{22} - f_{12}^2)}.$$

Since the second term in the denominator drops out (as it did in the above analysis with monopoly) it becomes clear that the remainder of the expression is exactly twice that of the monopoly or:

$$\frac{\partial P}{\partial P_1} = \frac{x_1}{Q}.$$

The change in the use of the substitute factor x_2 can also be seen using Cramer's rule:

$$\frac{\partial x_2}{\partial P_1} = \frac{-f_1 f_2 - g'Pf_{12}}{P(f_1^2 f_{22} + f_2^2 f_{11} - 2f_1 f_2 f_{12}) + P^2 g'(f_{11}f_{22} - f_{12}^2)}.$$

This is the equation used in the text to determine the change in the use of non-price fixed inputs brought about by an increase in the price of the price fixed input.

CHAPTER IV

ALTERNATIVES TO THE ILLINOIS BRICK RULE

This chapter argues that the Illinois Brick decision should be overruled by Congressional legislation, without at this stage specifying exactly what form this legislation should take. The chapter begins with a discussion of the proper goals of antitrust enforcement, efficiency and compensation. Earlier the efficiency goal was set by the minimization of the welfare losses due to undeterred violations plus the costs of enforcement. Section I discusses both the role of compensation in antitrust enforcement and the tradeoffs between compensation, deterrence, and the administrative costs of enforcement. Section II reviews the holding of the Illinois Brick decision in some detail. The next section attempts to show that Illinois Brick was not a necessary consequence of its precedents. In Section IV a comprehensive analysis is made of the possible advantages and disadvantages of Illinois Brick based on the efficiency and compensation criteria developed above. Section V discusses in much more detail the most serious single flaw in the Illinois Brick decision, the possibility that direct purchasers will not sue their suppliers. A simple proposal to overrule Illinois Brick is then made in Section VI. This proposal is shown to "strictly dominate" Illinois Brick, since it is shown to preserve all of the advantages enumerated above and to perform no worse, and in some cases much better, for all the disadvantages to Illinois Brick. At this point it is concluded that Illinois Brick should be overruled by Congress. Since there are a multitude of possible ways to overrule Illinois Brick, the proposal in Section VI being but a single one, Section VII discusses other possible solutions to the Illinois Brick problem. This last section ends with a discussion of the conditions under which each of these alternatives would be the most appropriate means to overturn Illinois Brick. These conditions are empirical propositions relating to compensation, deterrence, and the administrative costs of enforcement. While the empirical implications for compensation were discussed in Chapter III on incidence, the empirical questions relating to enforcement costs and deterrence are the subjects of Chapters V and VI respectively.

I. Framework for the Solution to the Illinois Brick Problem--
    Efficiency and Compensation

Any solution to the Illinois Brick problem should take into account the dual goals of the efficiency of enforcement and the compensation of antitrust victims. The efficiency goal is satisfied by minimizing the sum of the welfare losses attributable to undeterred violations plus the administrative costs of enforcement. As seen in Chapter II, penalties, rewards, and substantive procedures affecting the costs of litigation can theoretically be altered in such a way to achieve this minimum.

Defining a proper goal for compensation of antitrust injuries is considerably more difficult. There are three distinct issues for discussion. First, who must be compensated? Second, what is the proper level of compensation? Third, how do we weigh the costs of making the compensation versus the value of the compensation itself? This last question implicitly involves making a tradeoff between efficiency and compensation. These three questions are addressed sequentially below.

Which injured parties should be compensated for antitrust injuries? Section 4 of the Clayton Act states that "Any person who shall be injured in his business or property by reason of anything forbidden in the antitrust laws--" shall be able to sue and recover treble damages. While this language seems rather all inclusive, the courts have quite sensibly devised rules whereby undeserving plaintiffs are denied standing to sue. Considering the almost limitless ramifications on relative prices and quantities of a single antitrust violation, some limitation of standing seems advisable. Using either the "direct injury" test or the "target area" test to separate remote injuries from legitimate ones, the courts have denied recovery to shareholders, creditors, and employees of injured corporations and to lessors whose lessees were injured by some antitrust violations.[1] Yet on the other hand in Radovich v. National Football League, the Court held that "...Congress itself has placed the private antitrust litigant in a most favorable position through the enactment of §5 of the Clayton Act. In the face of such a policy this court should not add requirements to burden the private litigant beyond what is specifically set forth by Congress in those laws."[2]

It is not disputed here that some limitations on standing are necessary when the ramifications of a single price change are so broad. However,

---

[1] See generally, Daniel Berger and Roger Bernstein, "An Analytical Framework for Antitrust Standing," Yale Law Journal (April 1977), pp. 809-883.

[2] 352 U.S. 445, 454 (1957).

in light of the broad scope of the language of the Clayton Act and numerous liberal interpretations such as Radovich, it seems appropriate to devise a rule which will compensate at least those parties most seriously injured by antitrust violations involving chains of manufacturing or distribution. In Chapter III we saw that although direct purchasers and substitute factors of production may suffer some losses in profits and factor payments respectively, the major portion of the overcharge is usually passed on to the indirect purchaser/final consumer. Compensating these injured parties should be seen to promote the compensatory goals of the antitrust laws.

The amount of compensation is another potentially difficult question. Compensation for an injury suffered implies that one is made whole by the compensatory payment, yet the Clayton Act specifies that deserving plaintiffs be paid treble damages. The trebling provision can be thought of as a means to provide a sufficient payment to compensate for the risk of litigation, for attorney's fees,[3] and for the interest lost during the litigation period. On the other hand, the trebling could also be viewed as the proper incentive for private parties to help enforce the antitrust laws, or an inducement to provide a public good. From an efficiency viewpoint, an optimal reward is found where a reduction in such penalty adds to welfare losses exactly what it saves in enforcement costs and an increase in reward does the opposite, it adds to enforcement costs what it saves in welfare losses. For the purposes of this chapter we shall assume that the payment of treble damages satisfies the compensatory purposes of the antitrust laws.

---

[3] Attorneys are generally paid far more by their clients than is awarded by the courts as "reasonable attorneys fees."

The various relationships between the compensation goal and the goal of efficient enforcement must be kept in mind in fashioning antitrust enforcement policies. There is a tradeoff between efficient enforcement and the just compensation of victims of antitrust violations because the act of compensation consumes society's resources, and thus adds to the administrative costs of enforcement. The Supreme Court expressed itself clearly in Bigelow v. RKO Radio Pictures,[4] where it gave express approval to the "tendency of the courts to find some way in which damages can be awarded where a wrong has been done. Difficulty of ascertainment is no longer confused with the right of recovery for a proven invasion of the plaintiff's rights." Difficulties arise, however, where the costs of apportionment are so high relative to the total recovery that the effective level of compensation becomes minimal. Indeed, the costs of apportioning damages among the various parties at bar was a primary concern of the Illinois Brick court. In the Antibiotics[5] litigation a large settlement was made to several classes of plaintiffs in which consumers eventually received a distribution of $28 million and attorneys received over $40 million.[6] The major portion of the settlement fund was paid out in attorney's fees and the costs of notice to all class members. This example serves to illustrate that compensation is not a costless goal, but rather must be achieved to some extent at the expense of the efficiency of resource use.

The tradeoff between efficiency of enforcement and compensation

---

[4] 327 U.S. 251, 265-66 (1946).

[5] West Virginia v. Chas. Pfizer & Co. 440 F. 2d 1079 (2d Cir. 1971).

[6] Statement of Frederick Rowe, Senate Hearings, p. 81.

was recognized by Congress in its passage of the parens patriae provision of the Antitrust Improvements Act of 1976. First, in the amended Section 15(d) (of the Clayton Act) Congress legislated that "damages may be proved and assessed in the aggregate by statistical or sampling methods, by the computation of illegal overcharges, or by such other reasonable system of estimating aggregate damages...without the necessity of separately proving the individual claim of, or amount of damage to, persons on whose behalf the suit was brought." Later in Section 15(e) it states that the monetary relief may "be deemed a civil penalty by the court and deposited with the State as general revenues" (provided that each person has had a reasonable opportunity to secure his appropriate portion). Thus, in this legislation Congress has recognized that the calculation of individual damages and the payment of such damages to individuals is in itself a costly undertaking and has specified circumstances under which at the discretion of the court the compensatory goal should be sacrificed for the purposes of efficiency. The parens patriae provision was inspired in part by a growing recognition of the costliness and cumbersomeness of antitrust enforcement of the class action variety. This line of reasoning seems to imply that we are sacrificing too much in efficiency (the costs of enforcement) relative to the value of the compensation which remains after the various costs of suit are subtracted. Thus, while compensation remains a legitimate goal of antitrust enforcement, it should be remembered that it is not the only goal, and that in some cases it must be purchased at the expense of efficient enforcement.

The relationship between efficiency and compensation has yet another facet. Whereas we just discussed the tradeoff between the compensation of antitrust victims and the administrative costs of enforcement, the relationship between compensation and deterrence is of equal importance. This relationship can be seen most clearly if we redefine the compensation goal to minimize the <u>number</u> of <u>uncompensated</u> victims of antitrust violations. While the above tradeoff argument indicated that when the number of competing parties to be compensated rises, the administrative costs of enforcement also rise, it is also true that the number of uncompensated victims will fall as the deterrence of antitrust violators improves. Thus, from this perspective, there is a <u>positive</u> relationship between compensation and deterrence. When the efficiency goal is broken down into its two constituent parts--minimizing the sum of welfare losses due to undeterred violations and the costs of enforcement, it is seen that there is no tradeoff between the first component of efficiency and compensation; rather, increased deterrence helps compensation. It is only the administrative costs component of efficiency that involves a tradeoff with compensation.

Finally, it should be remembered that perfect compensation is never possible. Consumers who cease consuming a product due to its high price are very definitely injured, yet they would not have standing to sue antitrust violators simply because they do not purchase the higher priced items. Further we have seen that partly in the interests of the efficient allocation of judicial resources, several classes of parties are barred from collecting treble damages for antitrust injuries. Considering the possible tradeoff between efficiency and compensation, compensation of the victims of antitrust injuries seems to be one more instance where "the perfect is the enemy of the good." However, considering the overwhelming evidence that it is the indirect purchaser that is most injured by antitrust violations involving chains of distribution, the remainder of this dissertation will assume that the compensatory goal of the antitrust laws requires that indirect purchasers be compensated for injuries suffered. The next section reintroduces the subject of the Illinois Brick decision.

II. The Illinois Brick Decision

In Illinois Brick v. State of Illinois, the Supreme Court held that indirect purchasers cannot as a matter of law sue for treble damages. The Court relied heavily on Hanover Shoe v. United Shoe Machinery where the defendant attempted to escape liability for his wrongdoing by asserting that the plaintiff was not injured in his business or property since he passed on the overcharge to his own customers. The Court in Hanover Shoe, reasoned that the proof of passing on would involve long, complex, and expensive testimony. In addition, absent the ability of the plaintiffs to recover, the defendants may well have been able to escape liability completely since the plaintiff's customers, consumers of shoes, were not well disposed to bring suit. For these two reasons the Court in Hanover Shoe held that defendants could not as a matter of law introduce testimony to the effect that plaintiffs were not injured because they passed on the overcharge.

The Court in Illinois Brick was seriously concerned with the problem of multiple liability. This problem could arise if inconsistent judgments were arrived at in different courts. For example, multiple liability could arise if indirect purchasers in one court were allowed to prove that an overcharge had been passed on to them, while in another court the defendant facing a direct purchaser plaintiff, was not even allowed to attempt to prove what had been resolved in the first court. Due to this concern with the problem of multiple liability, the court decided first that whatever rule governed the admissability of passing on, it should be applied equally to plaintiffs and defendants. Thus, the second stage decision became: should indirect purchaser plaintiffs be precluded from bringing suit or should Hanover Shoe be overruled (or narrowly limited)?

Several factors prompted the Court to uphold Hanover Shoe and thus deny recovery to indirect purchasers. The Court recognized that the difficulties of analyzing price and output decisions for the purpose of proving that passing on has occurred are at least as great for plaintiffs as for defendants. It was concerned with the possibility that antitrust trials would become massively complicated multiparty litigations involving several layers of distribution. In addition, the Court felt that the purposes of deterring antitrust violators would be better served by concentrating the ability to sue in the direct purchaser. Otherwise by diffusing the benefits of bringing suit and by increasing the costs of litigation, the effectiveness of private antitrust would be weakened.

The plaintiffs in Illinois Brick argued that passing on should at least be permitted where middlemen resell goods without alteration and where contractors add a fixed percentage markup to the cost of their materials before submitting a bid. In both of these cases proof of pass on would be easy and the passing on was likely to have occurred. But the Supreme Court rejected attempts to carve out exceptions to the Hanover Shoe rule for particular types of markets. Instead it allowed for two more narrow exceptions to the direct purchaser rule: one where there is a cost plus contract,[7] an exception preserved from Hanover Shoe, and another where

---

[7] That this exception was intended to be narrow can be seen from the language of Illinois Brick, "But this Court in Hanover Shoe indicated the

the direct purchaser is owned or controlled by its customer.[8] Thus the law remains, at least until and unless the Congress chooses to overrule Illinois Brick, that indirect purchasers cannot, except in cases where the exceptions apply, bring suit against alleged antitrust violators to disgorge them of their profits.

III. Illinois Brick--A Necessary Consequence of Hanover Shoe?

This section will argue that Illinois Brick was not a necessary consequence of Hanover Shoe and the relevant legislative history of the antitrust laws. Rather, the opposite may have been the case. There were several precedents which could have influenced the court in deciding to allow indirect purchasers to sue antitrust violators. In addition, the legislative history of both the Sherman Antitrust Act and the new Antitrust Improvements Act of 1976 indicates very clearly that Congress intended that indirect purchasers would be able to sue violators.

Many of the lower courts prior to Illinois Brick had not read Hanover Shoe as precluding recovery to indirect purchasers. In deciding In re

---

narrow scope it intended for any exception to its rule barring pass-on defenses by citing, as the only example of a situation where the defense might be permitted, a preexisting cost-plus contract. In such a situation, the purchaser is insulated from any decrease in its sales as a result of attempting to pass on the overcharge, because its customer is committed to buying a fixed quantity regardless of price." 431 U.S. at 735-736. Thus, cost-plus pricing which is not formalized in a contract would not fall within the exception to the Illinois Brick rule.

[8] The actual language reads, "Another situation in which market forces have been superseded and the pass-on defense might be permitted is where the direct purchaser is owned or controlled by its customer. Cf. Perkins v. Standard Oil Co., In re Western Liquid Asphalt Cases (citations omitted)." 431 U.S. at 736 (in footnote). This exception is ambiguous since the cases cited immediately after the exception, Perkins and Western Liquid Asphalt, are cases where the direct purchaser is owned or controlled by its supplier, the alleged price fixer, not its customer.

Master Key Antitrust Litigation, a lower court held that "the attempt to transform a rejection of a defense because it unduly hampers antitrust enforcement into a reason for a complete refusal to entertain the claims of a certain class of plaintiffs seems an ingenious attempt to turn the decision (in Hanover Shoe) and its underlying rationale on its head."[9] In the Western Liquid Asphalt Cases the circuit court ruled that to deny State governments which purchased asphalt through paving contractors standing to prove that they were injured by overcharges from price fixing violations passed on to them would be to incorrectly read Hanover Shoe. The court held that passing on could be used offensively as a theory of recovery. Indeed, in the Senate Report on the Antitrust Improvements Act of 1976, which in part provided that the State Attorneys General could sue as parens patriae for damage done to its residents by reason of antitrust violations, concludes with the statement that "as between competing claimants within the chain of distribution...including consumers, the section 4C(a)(1) proviso is intended to assure that the monetary relief is properly allocated."[10] Congressman Rodino, one of the bill's co-sponsors, was quoted as saying that "if the intervening presence of such a middleman is to prevent recovery, the bill will be utterly meaningless."[11] In the same Senate report cited above, the Senate pointed directly to the Western Liquid Asphalt Cases in demonstrating good antitrust enforcement and directed the courts

---

[9] 1973-2 Trade Cas. 74,680 at 94,978-979 (D.C. Conn. 1973).

[10] U.S., Congress, Senate, Committee on the Judiciary, The Antitrust Improvements Act of 1976, S. Rept. 803 to accompany S. 1284, 94th Cong., 2d Sess., 1976, p. 45.

[11] Congressional Record, #10295 (Sept. 16, 1976).

to apply such a common sense approach in apportioning damages.[12]

In deciding Illinois Brick the Supreme Court could also have applied similar reasoning to that articulated in recent antitrust decisions in the area of price discrimination. In Perkins v. Standard Oil,[13] Clyde Perkins brought a treble damage suit against the defendant alleging that Standard Oil had charged him a higher price for his gasoline and oil than to Signal Oil who sold its product through an intervening subsidiary to a competitor of Perkins. In deciding that the intervening presence of middlemen was no basis upon which to deny recovery, the Court pointed to FTC v. Fred Meyer,[14] where it had held that a retailer who buys through a wholesaler could be considered a customer of the original supplier for the purposes of enforcing the Robinson Patman Act. In Perkins, the Court followed this precedent in stating that "to read 'customer' more narrowly in this section than we did in the section involved in Meyer would allow price discriminators to avoid the sanctions of the Act by the simple expedient of adding an additional link to the distribution chain." In deciding Illinois Brick, the Court could have made a similar argument. They could have reasoned that antitrust violators could avoid the sanctions of the antitrust laws by adding an additional "captive" link to the chain of distribution and thus remain immune to suit unless indirect purchasers were allowed to sue.

---

[12] "The Committee intention is to codify the holding of the 9th Circuit in In re Western Liquid Asphalt Cases," The Antitrust Improvements Act of 1976, p. 44.

[13] 395 U.S. 642 (1969).

[14] 390 U.S. 341 (1968).

IV. The Advantages and Disadvantages of Illinois Brick

If the advantages and disadvantages of the Illinois Brick decision are carefully laid out, especially when viewed in the context of the efficiency of enforcement and compensation goals cited above, they provide a convenient framework within which to compare the effects of Illinois Brick to those of possible alternatives. This section attempts to specify and further explore these advantages and disadvantages, thus providing the groundwork for comparison with other possible rules of recovery in treble damage suits.

Advantages of Illinois Brick

(1) Illinois Brick avoids the complication and expense of proving passing on, that is, establishing who has borne the burden of the overcharge. "But allowing indirect purchasers to recover using pass-on theories, even under the optimistic assumption...would transform treble-damage actions into massive multiparty litigations involving many levels of distribution and including large classes of ultimate consumers remote from the defendant."[15] The fact that the necessary proof of passing on may itself be costly detracts from the efficiency of antitrust enforcement for it directly increases the costs of litigation.[16] As we saw in Chapter II, unless such a reduction in the costs of litigation is accompanied by a tremendously large increase in the number of suits brought without a corresponding reduction in the number of antitrust violations, any reduction in the costs

---

[15] Illinios Brick, 431 U.S. 720 at 740.

[16] Closely related to the costliness of proving passing on is its inherent impracticality. Since a completely accurate determination of burden distribution would be impossible, the process is likely to be somewhat arbitrary.

of litigation makes us better off.

(2) Illinois Brick concentrates the ability to sue in the direct purchaser class. Both because of (1), that the direct purchaser will not have to contend with the costly passing on defense, and also because the expected value of recovery is both higher and more certain when the direct purchaser does not face the prospect of sharing his recovery with various indirect purchaser plaintiffs, the direct purchaser may be more willing to sue the price fixer and more capable of carrying the litigation to completion. Under Illinois Brick the direct purchaser can expect to recover 3J where J is the dollar value of the overcharge. In the event that passing on must be proven and there is one direct purchaser and one indirect purchaser (class), the two parties stand to share $(3J - C_{pp})$ where C_{pp} is the cost of proving whether and to what extent the burden of the overcharge has been passed on to the indirect purchaser. Thus, there are several reasons why the direct purchaser may be made more willing to sue the violator than would either party alone. Not only (1) is the total net amount to be recovered by the two parties lower than under Illinois Brick, but (2) the amount to be collected by either party alone is even lower, and (3) the certainty equivalent value is even lower still if the parties are risk averse. If plaintiffs have a threshold value of expected recovery below which the costs of litigation exceed the expected rewards, this threshold should fall under Illinois Brick since the costs of litigation would drop and the certainty of recovery would rise. At the same time this threshold drops expected recoveries would rise, therefore making litigation more likely, ceteris paribus.

(3) Multiple liability would be impossible under Illinois Brick. In the absence of Illinois Brick, defendants could theoretically be subject

to multiple liability if cases involving direct and indirect purchasers
allegedly injured by the same price fixer were pending in different courts
or at different times, <u>and</u> if the courts came to different conclusions
on the question of passing on. The costs and frequency of multiple liability are discussed in much greater detail in the next chapter. At this
point it is sufficient to note that whatever the costs to society of multiple liability under alternative standing rules, multiple liability would
be impossible under <u>Illinois Brick</u>.

(4) <u>Illinois Brick</u> may further the compensatory goal of antitrust
enforcement for two reasons. If the administrative costs of litigation
fall (say due to the elimination of the requirement that passing on be
proved), the <u>amount</u> to be compensated rises accordingly. Thus, to the
extent that (1) above is true, compensation would be improved. Secondly,
if the concentration of the right to sue and therefore its benefits helps
deter antitrust violations, the <u>number</u> of uncompensated victims may fall.[17]
Thus, to the extent that number (2) above has empirical validity, compensation will also be improved under <u>Illinois Brick</u>.

<u>Disadvantages of Illinois Brick</u>

(1) For a number of reasons the direct purchaser may be unwilling
to sue his supplier, the price fixer. Even Justice White in writing the
majority opinion in <u>Illinois Brick</u> stated, "We recognize that direct purchasers sometimes may refrain from bringing a treble-damage suit for fear
of disrupting relations with their suppliers. But on balance, and until
there are clear directions from Congress to the contrary, we conclude that

---

[17] For a reduction in the total number of uncompensated victims to occur, the increased deterrence of antitrust violators must be sufficient to more than outweigh the lack of compensation to indirect purchasers.

the legislative purpose in creating a group of 'private attorneys general' to enforce the antitrust laws under §4,...is better served by holding direct purchasers to be injured by the full amount of the overcharge...."[18] Indeed, not only are there good theoretical reasons why a direct purchaser may be unwilling to sue his supplier, but there is considerable evidence that this has in fact been the case in a variety of market situations. These reasons are elaborated in the next section and empirical evidence is presented in Chapter VI.

(2) Illinois Brick compensates the wrong party and fails to compensate the correct party in most instances. In Chapter III we investigated the conditions under which direct and indirect purchasers would be most injured by antitrust violations. When these results were applied to a sample of recent price fixing cases, it was found that in almost all cases the indirect purchaser bore the burden of antitrust injury. Thus in most instances under Illinois Brick, the direct purchaser receives a windfall recovery and the indirect purchaser receives nothing. This obviously frustrates the goal of compensation of antitrust injuries. It should be mentioned here that the fact that the use of proof of passing on does not guarantee correct compensation is not a reason to embrace Illinois Brick, since this decision effectively guarantees incorrect compensation in most cases.

(3) Potential price fixers may circumvent the intention of the Illinois Brick decision relatively easily, thus incurring unnecessary costs and sacrificing some deterrence. By adding another link in the chian of distribution, which he controls in some way, a price fixer may well be

---

[18] 431 U.S. 720, 746.

able to shield himself from treble damage actions. As indicated in Section II above, footnote 16 of Illinois Brick states that passing on may be used defensively (and thus offensively) where "the direct purchaser is owned or controlled by its customer." This footnote continues by citing a case where the direct purchaser is controlled by his supplier, not his customer.[19] As a result, unless this passage is interpreted liberally, defendants may well be able to escape liability by merely adding an additional link--such as a captive distributor--to the chain.

(4) The parens patriae provision of the Antitrust Improvements Act of 1976 is effectively nullified by Illinois Brick. Numerous state attorneys general have stated in Congressional testimony that about 90 to 95% of the purchases of their respective states are as indirect purchasers.[20] Many of the state attorneys general have been extremely active in a multitude of large treble damage actions during the last few years and there is considerable evidence that they will be even more active in the future. Thus, a valuable safety valve for antitrust enforcement is effectively lost under Illinois Brick. In addition to being independent instigators of antitrust actions, the state attorneys general could be effective "enforcers of last resort," making sure that price fixing is not profitable in those cases where the levels above have not sued.

The following section will discuss in somewhat more detail the potentially most serious problem brought about by the Illinois Brick decision --the possibility that direct purchasers will not sue their suppliers.

---

[19] 431 U.S. at 736.

[20] See for instance the testimony of Chauncey Browning, the Chairman of the Antitrust Committee of the National Association of Attorneys General, in Senate Hearings, p. 103.

V. Why Direct Purchasers May Not Sue Their Suppliers

No profit maximizing company would willingly forgo the opportunity of obtaining treble damages unless the costs of doing so are likely to outweigh the rewards. This situation may occur when the price fixing is profitable to the direct purchaser, when the price fixer exerts some sort of control over the direct purchaser and is even more likely when both conditions are met simultaneously.

In situations where the direct purchaser faces relatively inelastic demand and uses a fixed percentage markup pricing rule, he profits rather than suffers by the advent of price fixing. This profitability of passing on an overcharge coupled with the costs and risks of litigation may make a direct purchaser unwilling to bring a treble damage action. In such instances, in the absence of indirect purchaser suits, the antitrust violator would be left with the fruits of his violation.[21]

Another instance where a direct purchaser may be unwilling to sue his supplier would be where the supplier exerts some form of control over the direct purchaser. The control need not be complete ownership. It may be more subtle such as the ability to exercise financial pressure through a restriction of credit terms. Thus, while one might aruge that any retaliation would be further evidence of a violation, the sublety of

---

[21] This is one of the few instances where perverse incentives may be operative. Above we argued that a risk averse party would be unwilling to forgo certain present losses in the form of lost profits due to overcharges for uncertain future gains in the form of treble damages. But here there are no present losses to be sacrificed, for we have argued that the price fixing may be profitable to the direct purchaser if the demand is very inelastic and a cost plus percentage markup pricing system is utilized. If perverse incentives are ever operative, this would be a possible instance. However, if direct purchasers do not sue their suppliers, there is no reason to believe that they are postponing suit. Rather they may be forgoing the opportunity to sue completely.

possible reactions by the price fixer may make this argument invalid. Not only could the defendant cause a deterioration or detraction of favorable credit terms, but he could arrange for goods to be delivered more slowly, "mistakes" to be made, or various and sundry other problems for his recalcitrant customer which are difficult to prove in court. In particular, direct purchasers may fear the retaliation of their suppliers most when there are characteristic shortages in the industry and where their inventory positions are crucial to profitability. However, any situation where the goodwill of a supplier has become an important intangible asset may cause a wary direct purchaser to refrain from suing.

Where both factors are present, where price fixing is both profitable (or at least not injurious) to the direct purchaser and where there exists some control by the price fixer over the direct purchaser or an intangible asset of goodwill between them, failure to sue the price fixer may be even more likely. Again, in such instances the antitrust violators would be able to perpetrate their violations with little risk of loss if indirect purchasers were unable to bring suit.

It should be mentioned that the ability of one party to bring a class action representing numerous other parties may be a countervailing influence. In such cases, provided that the individual class members do not opt out of the litigation, only a single party need bring suit in order for the entire direct purchaser class to recover. Chapter VI below deals directly with the actual as opposed to the theoretical effects of class actions on the deterrence provided by direct purchasers.

VI. A Proposal to Amend the Statute of Limitations

This section will describe one proposal to overrule Illinois Brick.[22] After a brief description of the proposal it will be shown to preserve all four of the advantages of the Illinois Brick decision listed and explained above. In addition, it will perform at least as well and in some cases much better for each of the disadvantages described above. It will then be concluded that the Illinois Brick decision should be overruled by Congress. The exact shape of the new rules for recovery must await a comparison between this one proposal and various alternative methods of overturning Illinois Brick. Several of these alternatives are discussed later in this chapter. The following two chapters then discuss and test certain empirical propositions in order to decide between the various ways of overturning Illinois Brick.

Assume first that there is only one direct purchaser and one indirect purchaser in the chain of manufacturing and distribution. As with Illinois Brick, the direct purchaser would at first have the exclusive right to sue his supplier, the antitrust violator, for treble damages without having to prove that he did not pass on the overcharge. Rather, the direct purchaser would be entitled to treble the value of the overcharge whether or not he was actually injured. This period of exclusive right to sue would expire at the end of the normal four year statute of limitations or one year after the indirect purchaser filed a notice of intention to sue the price fixer with an appropriate authority, which ever comes first. One year after this date the indirect purchaser would gain the

---
[22] A similar proposal was made by Stephen Babb in "The Effect of Hanover Shoe on the Offensive Use of the Passing-on Doctrine," 46 Southern California Law Review, pp. 98-116.

exclusive right to sue the price fixer for triple the full value of the overcharge, again without the necessity of having to prove that the overcharge was passed on to him. In this fashion, should the indirect purchaser either fail to discover the price fixing conspiracy or fail to file notice, the direct purchaser's exclusive right to recovery would thereby be extended to four years. However, should the direct purchaser be unwilling to sue his supplier, the indirect purchaser would gain the exclusive right to sue after a short period. The normal four year statute of limitations could still apply to govern the total period wherein the price fixer would be liable for damages, and it could still apply retrospectively. Therefore, using this scheme one party would always have an exclusive right to recovery without the necessity of proving that passing on did or did not occur.

The same principle would apply when there is more than one level of indirect purchaser. Any party discovering the violation and wishing to recover would file a notice of intention to sue. This party would have the exclusive right to the recovery in one year unless a party closer to the price fixer filed a notice (or a suit in the case of the direct purchaser) in the interim.[23]

This scheme of using a modified statute of limitations for the purposes of giving one party the exclusive right to sue without the necessity of having to prove passing on can be shown to be superior to the results of the Illinois Brick decision by using the framework established above. The next several paragraphs will compare this solution to Illinois Brick

---

[23] A fine could be assessed against any party who fails to bring suit after filing the required notice in order to discourage this behavior.

using the eight criteria listed and discussed above.

Advantages

(1) As with *Illinois Brick* no proof of passing would ever be necessary under this scheme. This avoids the complications, costs and arbitrariness inherent in such proof.

(2) The ability to sue would still be concentrated in one party. Thus the argument used by Justice White in his majority opinion, that in the absence of *Illinois Brick* the higher costs of litigation and the diffusion of benefits would erode the willingness and ability to sue and recover, would not be valid. With the modified statue of limitations scheme the right to sue is also concentrated. Therefore, this advantage is also preserved.

(3) As with *Illinois Brick* multiple liability is impossible, since only one party at a time has the right to recover. This right to recover precludes duplicative recovery by others.

(4) To the extent that the costs of proving passing on and of multiparty litigation reduce the value of compensation, *Illinois Brick* promotes compensation of victims. Since the proposal outlined above eliminates the need for any such costs to be expended ((1) above) it preserves this compensatory advantage of *Illinois Brick*. In addition, to the extent that the concentration of the ability to sue, (2) above, increases deterrence, it decreases the number of uncompensated victims. Since our proposal also concentrates the ability to sue in one party, this aspect of compensation is also preserved.

Disadvantages

(1) If for reasons of the profitability of price fixing or of unwillingness to disturb a cozy relationship with a supplier (or both), the direct purchaser were unwilling to sue his supplier under Illinois Brick, no suit would be brought, the violator would retain his ill gotten gains, and other potential violators would not be deterred. Yet under the new proposal, indirect purchasers would have ample opportunity to substitute their own claims against the antitrust violator. To the extent that those parties actually injured are more likely to bring suit, ceteris paribus, indirect purchasers are more likely to fill the vacuum in precisely those instances where direct purchasers do not sue--where there is inelastic demand and a cost plus percentage markup pricing system. Indirect purchasers would also be available plaintiffs when the direct purchaser was controlled in some fashion by the antitrust violator. Even if no indirect purchaser stepped in to sue where direct purchasers had failed to do so, a result totally contrary to fact as we shall see in Chapter VI, this scheme would perform no worse than does Illinois Brick on this score.

(2) The modified statute of limitations plan is more likely to compensate the correct party. If the direct purchaser is the party truly injured, he still can recover his rightful treble damage payment. If it is the indirect purchaser that is truly injured, this scheme provides a possibility for correct compensation and therefore is superior. This is especially true, if as stated above, an injured party is more likely to file suit and therefore to recover. If direct and indirect purchasers both suffer injury the argument still applies. If the direct purchaser does file suit, we have the Illinois Brick situation. If not, at least the indirect purchaser has a chance to be compensated.

(3) It was pointed out above that under *Illinois Brick* a price fixer could possibly add a "captive" distributor to his chain of distribution and barring the applicability of footnote 16, be free of the challenge of recoupment of losses. No such behavior attempting to circumvent the intent of *Illinois Brick* would obviously be possible under the new proposal. More importantly, no harm would result if potential plaintiffs attempted to keep secret their intention to file suit. On the contrary, the possibility of such secrecy on the part of an indirect purchaser may produce positive benefits. If we make the assumption that it is always easier for the direct purchaser to detect a violation than for an indirect purchaser to do so, then the only conditions under which secrecy could affect the outcome would be where the direct purchaser was postponing suit --a perverse incentives case. Although we have shown above in Chapter II that perverse incentives are probably not empirically common, this scheme would serve to help further discourage them to the extent that they exist. If direct purchasers *were* postponing suit in order to collect more damages, they may be penalized by losing their opportunity to sue to the indirect purchaser. To the extent that they perceive the possibility of this loss, perverse incentives would be ameliorated.

(4) Under the new proposal the safety valve of the *parens patriae* and proprietary actions by state attorneys general would be preserved. This is particularly valuable where direct purchasers are unwilling to sue and the only other possible party is a diffuse class of consumers, the value of whose individual purchases is very small. Under this scheme the attorneys general can step in where no other parties are suing, thus extracting the overcharges from the price fixer who would otherwise have benefited from his illegal actions.

Since this plan works at least as well and sometimes better than
Illinois Brick as measured by all eight criteria established above, _Illinois
Brick_ should be overruled by Congress. The next section will enumerate
and discuss some other possibilities for overruling the _Illinois Brick_
decision.

VII. Other Possible Solutions to the Illinois Brick Dilemma

Apart from the admittedly simplistic and somewhat arbitrary solution just presented, there exist numerous ways in which the _Illinois Brick_ decision could be overruled by Congress. The following possibilities should not be considered comprehensive, nor should they be considered mutually exclusive, combinations are of course possible. Together with each possibility is a brief qualitative discussion of the economic circumstances in which they would be most appropriate (or inappropriate). A more detailed discussion of the merits of each proposal will await quantitative assessment of the relevant parameters in the following chapters.

(1) The Congress could recreate the distinction held in some of the circuits prior to _Illinois Brick_ between middlemen and consumers of the price fixed good. In cases where the price fixed good was sold _without alteration_, passing on would be permitted, whereas where the price fixed good was an input to another production process, passing on would _not_ be permitted. Such a distinction would further the goals of the antitrust laws to the extent that the efficiency and compensatory reasons militating for and against _Illinois Brick_ divided precisely according to the type of market use of the price fixed good delineated above. More specifically, this distinction would be totally appropriate if the true incidence of the overcharge were accurately predictable using the middleman/consumer

distinction, _and_ the injured party is the one who is more willing and able to sue the price fixer. It would be relatively _more_ appropriate:

    (a) the less likely middlemen direct purchasers are to sue their suppliers and the more likely _their_ customers are to sue,

    (b) the more likely consumer direct purchasers are to sue their suppliers and the less likely their customers are to sue,

    (c) the more the distinction between middlemen and consumer direct purchasers reflects the distinction between truly injured parties, and

    (d) the less costly is the proof of passing on for middlemen direct purchasers, and therefore the less the litigation threshold rises with such proof.

It should be mentioned that this distinction which considers only the _use_ to which the price fixed good is put in deciding the rules of recovery, constitutes a _per se_ rule which therefore is somewhat arbitrary in its imposition. The costs of such a rule must be outweighed by the benefits sufficiently to justify the arbitrariness of the rule.

    (2) Congress could overrule both _Illinois Brick_ and _Hanover Shoe_ allowing both offensive and defensive use of the pass-on. This solution would be an improvement upon the middleman/consumer distinction to the extent that such a delineation does not accurately reflect either injury, willingness and ability to sue or both. This solution would be relatively more appropriate the greater the unwillingness of direct purchasers to sue their suppliers, the smaller the cost of proving passing on, and the less the effect of such proof would have on the litigation threshold of potential plaintiffs.

    (3) _Illinois Brick_ and _Hanover Shoe_ could remain law but an amend-

mend could be enacted by Congress which would allow state attorneys general to sue both in their proprietary capacities and as parens patriae even when their purchases and those of the citizens of their states are indirect. This solution is more appropriate to the extent that proof of passing on entails expensive multiparty litigation which raises the litigation threshold, yet preserves the safety valve of parens patriae suits in the event that direct purchasers do not sue their suppliers. Parens patriae suits are able to circumvent many of the costly and time consuming procedures of ordinary class actions and thus may conserve on the administrative costs of enforcement. This solution is also more appropriate to the extent that the state attorneys general are active litigants in antitrust treble damage actions and can substitute their own suits for other indirect purchaser suits not brought. The next chapter details the recent activity of the various states and assesses the extent to which their participation as indirect purchasers would help antitrust enforcement.

(4) Congress could overrule only Illinois Brick. Then the defendant would be unable to use the passing on defense, yet indirect purchasers could still sue. This alternative approximates the prevailing situation during 1968-1977 in several circuits.

This solution would be inferior to one where both Illinois Brick and Hanover Shoe are overruled, to the extent that we worry about multiple liability. If indirect purchasers are equally well disposed to prove that they have suffered injury under these two solutions, then multiple liability would be more likely where the direct purchaser faces fewer obstacles to recovery. Where Hanover Shoe is preserved, and thus where defendants cannot use the passing on defense, direct purchaser recovery and therefore multiple liability would be more likely.

This solution would be superior to one which overrules _Hanover Shoe_ in situations where direct purchasers may have trouble proving that they _absorbed_ the overcharge, but where indirect purchasers are unavailable for suit. Where indirect purchasers are not disposed to bring suit, the availability of the passing on defense may hurt antitrust enforcement.

The list of alternatives to the _Illinois Brick_ rule just described is not exhaustive; other solutions are certainly possible. Each listed alternative is relatively more appropriate under certain circumstances. These circumstances naturally fall into one of three categories.
(1) _Compensation_: Which parties are most injured by antitrust violations? This question was dealt with in Chapter III above. (2) _Deterrence_: Which parties are most willing and able to bring antitrust suits? This crucially important question is discussed in Chapter VI below. (3) _The Administrative Costs of Enforcement_: How great are the costs of proving passing on, of multiparty litigation, and also of multiple liability? This last question is discussed next in Chapter V. The empirical determinations to be made in the next two chapters serve to determine the most appropriate way to overrule the _Illinois Brick_ decision.

CHAPTER V

THE ADMINISTRATIVE COSTS OF ENFORCEMENT

This chapter deals with the administrative costs of enforcing the antitrust laws under various possible rules of standing. It also deals with a closely related issue--the efficiency of antitrust enforcement by the various state attorneys general who are considered private parties under the antitrust laws. Before discussing the substantive issues of this chapter, it would be appropriate to summarize our discussion thus far in order to give perspective and direction to the remainder of the dissertation. We began in Chapter II by discussing the issue of antitrust enforcement as a public good and as such, the optimal level of enforcement. When the efficiency of public and private enforcement was compared, we found private enforcement to be a relatively efficient complement to public enforcement of the antitrust laws. We then proceeded in Chapter III to discuss the compensatory implications of <u>Illinois Brick</u>. This was accomplished by examining some simple partial equilibrium models of incidence to determine the conditions under which a price fixed overcharge would be borne by various parties in the chain of manufacturing or distribution of a price fixer--the <u>Illinois Brick</u> fact setting. Then by applying these models to a sample of price fixing cases brought by the Department of Justice in a recent period, the real world incidence of these price fixed overcharges was determined. Chapter IV discussed the _Illinois Brick_ decision in much more detail and concluded, by comparing its results to those of another possible rule of recovery, that the decision should be legislatively overruled. There are numerous ways for Congress to overturn _Illinois Brick_, some of which were specified in the last chapter. It is now our task to delineate the advantages and disadvantages of alternative courses of Congressional action.

We previously determined a set of objectives to be fulfilled in deciding the best rule to govern antitrust standing, efficiency and equity (or deterrence and compensation, taking into account the costs of enforcement). Now we also have a set of possible alternatives to _Illinois Brick_ described briefly in the last chapter. We have seen that each of these alternatives is more or less appropriate as a substitute for _Illinois Brick_ depending on the value of certain parameters and the extent to which certain assertions made by the Supreme Court have empirical validity. The empirical questions to be examined in this chapter all relate to the administrative costs of enforcing the antitrust laws under various possible standing rules. Many observers have criticized the complexity and unmanageability of private antitrust litigation. Section I reviews these arguments, discusses possible reforms, and also discusses the extent to which antitrust enforcement under the _Illinois Brick_ rule and alternative rules of standing consume scarce judicial and private resources. Section II deals with both the costs and likelihood of multiple liability. The third section discusses the recent rapid growth in antitrust activity by the state attorneys general, the comparative efficiency of state and non-state private enforcement and the implications of state enforcement for the decision to overturn _Illinois Brick_.

I. Complexity and Manageability of Antitrust Litigation

Many commentators have criticized the length, complexity, unmanageability and in addition, the possibilities for harassment inherent in private antitrust litigation.[1] These criticisms are particularly harsh when directed against class actions. Some of these same observers have concluded from such an assessment that the Illinois Brick decision brings sanity to the enforcement of the antitrust laws, since any other rule of recovery would further complicate already costly and complex cases and thus further crowd court dockets. These major criticisms will be first discussed and then their implications for the overruling of Illinois Brick will be examined.

(1) Length--Antitrust actions (both public and private) are extraordinarily lengthy and costly proceedings both to the parties involved and to the court system as a whole. The median time from filing to the disposition of antitrust cases concluded in fiscal 1977 was 16 months, compared to the length of civil rights, insurance, copyright and all U.S. cases of 10, 9, 6, and 7 months respectively. For those cases which went to trial the median length of antitrust cases was 44 months, as compared to 16, 16, 38, and 16 respectively for the four categories named above. Whereas only about 1.3% of all civil cases filed were antitrust cases, they represented about 5% of all cases pending for more than three years as of June 30, 1977.[2] By almost any available measure, antitrust cases are extremely lengthy and therefore probably more expensive than other

---

[1] See, for example, the testimony of Samuel Murphy, in Senate Hearings, pp. 173-188, and also Milton Handler and Michael Blechman, "Antitrust and the Consumer Interest: The Fallacy of Parens Patriae and A Suggested New Approach," 85 Yale Law Journal, pp. 626-676.

[2] Annual Report of the Director of the Administrative Office of the United States Courts, 1977, various tables.

litigation.

(2) Delays--To some extent the great length of antitrust cases can be attributed to the incentives of parties to delay the disposition of these cases. John Shenefield, the Assistant Attorney General for antitrust enforcement, in a major speech urging the attempt to find ways to shorten complex antitrust litigation, attributed such length to the incentives of defendants to postpone all stages of the litigation, the tendency of some litigants to overtry cases, and in addition the possibility that some judges may lose control of their cases.[3] The first phenomenon is illustrated clearly in the IBM case (although not a private case). IBM would not agree to the proposal of the United States to continue the current trial with a new judge in the event that Judge Edelstein dies before the case is completed, but rather wished to postpone the entire process by beginning a new trial.[4]

(3) Minimal Compensation--Private antitrust actions brought in the form of class actions have been particularly criticized because of the enormous administrative costs involved and thus the minimal value of consumer compensation possible with the remainder of the proceeds. The attorneys' fees and the very sizable costs of notice of parties may erode substantially the amount available for compensation to injured parties.[5] According to Frederick Rowe, the principal attorney for the Grocery Manufacturers of America, in one of the largest group of settlements in the

---

[3]Bureau of National Affairs, Antitrust and Trade Regulation Reporter (henceforth ATRR), Nov. 3, 1977.

[4]New York Times, September 30, 1977, p. D1.

[5]See generally, Handler and Blechman, pp. 626-676.

Antibiotics Cases, the parties received $28 million while $40 million was paid in costs and attorneys fees.[6]

(4) *Complexity of Multiparty Litigation*--In testimony to both the relevant House and Senate Subcommittees on the legislation to overturn the Illinois Brick decision, Samuel Murphy described the almost unbelievable complexity of the tetracycline litigation. This litigation at one time was comprised of 166 cases, most of which were brought as large class actions, seeking treble damages based on the charge that the alleged conspiracy of five pharmaceutical companies to raise and fix prices on tetracycline and other broad spectrum antibiotics injured them in their business or property. Cases were brought not only by classes representing wholesalers, retailers and final consumers but by numerous other parties as well. These included private hospitals as representatives of nationwide classes, by 49 out of 50 states on behalf of themselves and of consumers and governmental purchasers within their states, by insurance companies, by Blue Cross, by union welfare trust funds, and by the Federal government both for its own purchases and for monies paid out to the states and hospitals under Medicaid, Medicare and other programs. In addition, antibiotics are also used as animal feed supplements, thus there was a "veterinary" chain of distribution as well. Here suits were brought by wholesalers, distributors, feed mills, feed lot operators, veterinarians and groups of poultry, cattle, swine and mink raisers![7] It is not surprising that Mr. Murphy is in favor of the retention of Illinois Brick.

---

[6] Senate Hearings, p. 81.

[7] Testimony of Samuel Murphy, House Hearings, pp. 177-80.

(5) <u>Manageability</u>--Closely related to the issue above is the manageability of large class actions in another sense. In <u>Boshes</u> v. <u>General Motors</u>,[8] the court ruled that although indirect purchasers had <u>standing</u> to bring their class action, the class could not be certified on the grounds of size and of the complexities of individual proof of damages. If passing on had to be proven in each individual case, this would clearly increase the complexity of the litigation.

(6) <u>Harassment</u>--There is a widespread notion that undeserving plaintiffs may occasionally bring groundless suits against large corporations hoping for a settlement. The incidence of harassment is exacerbated to the extent that attorneys seeking large contingency fee payments "solicit" potential plaintiffs who otherwise would not have initiated treble damage litigation. This phenomenon is likely to be more prevalent where the law is unclear and where there is tremendous uncertainty attached to the probable outcome should the two parties end up in court. A recent survey of federal judges made by an administrative arm of the federal court system concluded that a majority of federal judges feel that corporate defendants buy peace through settlement rather than risk a trial on the merits because of the great cost of such a trial and the enormous size of the potential liability.[9] Thus, at least according to these judges, the possibility for harassment is ever present. It can perhaps be argued that such harassment is lessened under the <u>Illinois Brick</u> rule as there are fewer parties to do the harassing.

---

[8] 59 F.R.D. 589 (N.D. Ill. 1973). The proposed class consisted of between 30 and 40 million car buyers.

[9] ATRR, Sept. 29, 1977.

(7) _Growing Distrust of Class Actions_--Perhaps in response to all of the above substantive complaints, there seems to be a growing disenchantment with the effects of class action litigation. A most vocal Congressional opponent of class actions, Charles Wiggins, indicated recently that class actions "are maintained by and for attorneys," that they "do very little to compensate consumers for economic losses," and that they present a "very real" danger of overburdening the courts.[10]

These arguments taken together lead many to conclude that without the simplification and certainly of _Illinois Brick_, each of the problems underlying the complexity and unmanageability of antitrust litigation would be exacerbated. Therefore, the reasoning goes, overruling _Illinois Brick_ would be a grave mistake. Richard Posner recently concluded that,

> If _Illinois Brick_ is overruled, if private antitrust enforcement is channeled into the multitiered class action mold, and if the courts dismiss such actions as unmanageable, then even the most ardent proponent of private antitrust damage action may some day long for the return of _Illinois Brick_.[11]

It should first be mentioned that although the above arguments appear to be severe indictments of the complexity and unmanageability of large, multiparty, class action antitrust litigation, the conclusion that _Illinois Brick_ is a wise decision does not follow, at least on these grounds. To make such an inference would be to confuse total benefits and costs with marginal benefits and costs. Just because the total amount of antitrust "complexity" is inordinately high, it does not follow that any addition to this "complexity" for the purposes of equity and perhaps an increase

---

[10] ATRR, Oct. 20, 1977.

[11] Statement of Richard Posner, _House Hearings_, p. 195.

in deterrence would bring more costs than benefits. The marginal benefits may well exceed the marginal costs brought about by this increased "complexity" of allowing indirect purchasers to sue. Further, as we shall soon see, it is not at all clear that this marginal "complexity" will materialize to the extent predicted. Instead we may well see tremendous complications arising from the ambiguities of the Illinois Brick decision itself.

Secondly, looking at the _total_ costs of complex antitrust litigation, due to the lengthy delays, possible harassment, and the difficulties of complex multiparty litigation, Illinois Brick may be both an arbitrary and inefficient way of addressing the problem of administrative costs, not a minimum cost solution. Other proposals which attack the complexity, manageability, or harassment problems directly are much more likely to decrease the administrative cost component of enforcement while assuring equitable treatment of parties and maintaining, or even increasing, the incentives to sue violators. In particular, the modified statute of limitations scheme explained above was shown to preserve all the advantages of Illinois Brick while at the same time probably increasing the deterrence of antitrust violators. There may be far more efficient ways to reduce the costs of antitrust enforcement by addressing these problems directly than by eliminating the ability of most parties to sue for treble damages.

The Carter Administration has developed two distinct approaches for the purposes of simplification and reform of antitrust and other civil litigation, both of which would address the problems described above. The first is a new Blue Ribbon Panel created by executive order to study in part ways to simplify and shorten complex antitrust litigation. The second is a legislative proposal for the reform of class actions.

President Carter's new Antitrust Commission which began its work in June of 1978 was set up to discuss the dual issues of handling major cases and antitrust immunities.[12] It will discuss, among other things, the possibility of shortening trials by various means such as making changes in the rules of discovery and by granting judges the authority to penalize delay tactics of the various parties.[13]

In addition, the administration has prepared draft legislation for reforming class action procedures. One of the purposes of such legislation would be to further deter instances of illegal acts which produce pervasive small injury but where the individual damages are not sufficient to initiate action. The legislation is also intended to help provide redress without the current very expensive procedures inherent in class action litigation; hence, the manageability of cases should improve.

The administration's proposed reform assumes two different forms depending on the size of the individual injury. Where individual injury is small (less than $500 per person), it is assumed that the proper incentives to form a class and to file suit, give proper notice, and carry the suit to completion may be lacking. Most such small suits would be taken over by state or federal officials and thereby become "public penalty procedures." This change would serve the dual purpose of drastically reducing costs of suit by permitting the use of statistical techniques to

---

[12] The membership of this panel consists of John Shenefield, the Assistant Attorney General for Antitrust; Michael Pertchuk, the chairman of the Federal Trade Commission; Alfred Kahn, then the chairman of the Civil Aeronautics Board; Chauncey Browning, the chairman of the National Association of Attorneys General; Clyde Atkins, federal district judge; ten Senators and Congressmen including Edward Kennedy and Peter Rodino, the chairmen of the relevant Senate and House antitrust subcommittees, and seven prominent individuals from the private sector.

[13] ATRR, Nov. 24, 1977; May 25, 1978.

aggregate injury and by easing the notice requirements to involved parties, and also of drastically reducing the possibility of any harassment suits. The latter reduction occurs because federal or state officials can merely drop a case if they feel it was brought merely to harass some party. Public penalty actions would also reduce or eliminate the problem of manageability articulated in Boshes v. General Motors since passing on would not have to be proven in each individual case. In addition, the successful private plaintiff who originated the treble damage suit would recover an incentive reward right off the top of the penalty money in all public procedures. He would receive 20% of the first $25,000 and 10% of the next $50,000. This reward would presumably provide a much greater incentive to bring suit to a potential plaintiff who is damaged only by a small amount, thereby helping to internalize the externality he confers upon the other members of his class.[14]

Where the individual damages exceed $500 per person, it is assumed in the proposed legislation that adequate incentives exist to bring suit and bear the costs of notice. The reform intended for these suits where larger individual damages are involved concerns providing a greater disincentive to filing undeserving claims. To this end a preliminary hearing would be conducted at an early stage of the litigation where the prevailing party would be paid its attorney's fees (up to a limit). Harassment actions or other undeserving claims would be penalized almost from the outset.[15]

Without discussing the merits or demerits of the particular features

---

[14] ATRR, Dec. 8, 1977.

[15] ATRR, Dec. 8, 1977.

of the two proposals above, it should be clear that they directly address the issues of the length of antitrust suits, the reasons for delay, the incentives for harassment, the tremendous costs which eat away at compensation and therefore the general spectrum of problems giving rise to criticisms of the complex antitrust litigation, particularly where class actions are concerned. The fact that these solutions may be imperfect is irrelevant. These proposals or any others which provide demonstrable improvements in administrative efficiency without any (predictable) side effects are to be vastly preferred to an arbitrary denial of standing to classes of clearly deserving plaintiffs. This is particularly true if the arbitrary denial of standing does no better in solving the problem of administrative inefficiency but at the same time is demonstrably inequitable and decreases antitrust deterrence as well. Manageability or judicial efficiency is therefore not a sufficient reason to choose one solution over another to the Illinois Brick problem when other less costly reforms are available.

The Comparative Costs of Illinois Brick and Its Alternatives

We indicated above that some proponents of Illinois Brick defend this decision precisely because it prevents costly, complex and unmanageable antitrust litigation from becoming more costly, more complex and more unmanageable. This defense of Illinois Brick was criticized for two distinct reasons. First, it is the marginal changes in costs and benefits brought about by any given policy change that is relevant in making a decision as to whether or not to implement the change. Secondly, to the extent that the total costs of antitrust enforcement are too high, we must search for the least expensive way to reduce these enforcement costs, in terms of the alternatives forgone. Several examples indicated that there are probably less costly ways to reduce the costs of antitrust enforcement than the rather crude instrument of Illinois Brick. The solutions being considered or proposed by the President's new Antitrust commission and his class action reform bill address all the concerns articulated by critical observers of complex antitrust litigation except for one--the costs of proving passing on (and its consequent effects on the incentives to sue).

A sensible framework for deciding on a rule to overturn Illinois Brick would involve a combination of the two approaches above. All exogenous changes in rules, procedures, and penalties which reduce the total costs of enforcement and are likely to be implemented should be assumed. Then a comparison of the marginal gains and losses of particular changes in standing rules would indicate the desirability of implementing these changes. To illustrate this approach let us compare the costs and benefits derived by changing from an Illinois Brick rule to one where indirect purchasers may sue to recover damages.

The repeal of the Illinois Brick decision would put private antitrust enforcement back to its approximate status during the 1968-77 period between the Hanover Shoe and Illinois Brick opinions. (If Hanover Shoe is also repealed the pre-1968 period would be the appropriate one.) The costs of proving passing on encountered in these earlier periods should be compared not with the costlessness of the proof of pass on resulting from Illinois Brick, but rather with the other costs that Illinois Brick introduces. The following paragraphs discuss first the costs of proving passing on, and then the "other" costs which may be introduced by Illinois Brick.

It is difficult to accurately estimate the true costs to society of proving the extent to which passing on occurs, that is, apportioning damages among the various plaintiffs claiming damages from the same defendant(s). However, the fact that accurate assessment may be impossible should not deter us from making reasonable estimates. Numerous witnesses have testified in Congressional Hearings on <u>Illinois Brick</u> that once defendants are removed from the litigation, plaintiffs are very quickly able to apportion the available damages among themselves. For example the Assistant Attorney General of the State of California stated that,

> I think the amount of time that has been spent by the district judges addressing that specific question, the question of allocation between the various groups, the potential claimants on a multi-tier system, has been days if not hours. It simply has not been a time consuming process with the district courts largely because the plaintiff groups have resolved these questions among themselves.
> ......
> Once you take the defendant out of the process--which is what section 4D does--then you do not get the confusion and the stalling and the rest of it....Then things run very smoothly.[16]

If the testimony of this and other witnesses is to be taken seriously, then one must conclude that the costs of apportioning damages among the various plaintiffs making claims resulting from the same violation will not be overwhelmingly burdensome.[17] These costs of proving passing on which will result if <u>Illinois Brick</u> is overruled by Congress should be

---

[16] Statement of Michael Spiegel, <u>Senate Hearings</u>, p. 111.

[17] Admittedly, these estimates of the costs of proving passing-on do not cover instances where there is only one level of plaintiff claiming damages, but only holds where there are multiple levels of plaintiffs claiming their share of the same fund. However, in the former case one might argue that where liability has already been proved <u>and</u> where there is only one level of plaintiff claiming damages, no passing on proof is necessary at all; rather, deterrence <u>requires</u> that the one plaintiff be compensated. This issue will be dealt with in the last chapter.

compared to their alternative--to the costs that Illinois Brick introduces. The source of the additional costs likely to be introduced by Illinois Brick is the probable litigation concerning the two exceptions to the Illinois Brick rule--the ownership or control exception and the cost plus contract.

Footnote 16 of the Illinois Brick decision states that

> Another situation in which market forces have been superseded and the pass on defense might be permitted is where the direct purchaser is owned or controlled by its customer. Cf. Perkins v. Standard Oil, In re Western Liquid Asphalt Cases. (citations omitted).[18]

In both cases cited as examples of this exception, the direct purchaser was owned or controlled by the defendant, not by the indirect purchaser. There is likely to be considerable litigation concerning the Supreme Court's intention as to where the ownership or control must originate. Thus many of the benefits of the simplicity of the direct purchaser rule may not materialize, at least until this point is settled.

In addition there may be many more instances of questions relating to the meaning of ownership or control which have to be litigated. While it is recognized that complete ownership is unnecessary to fall within the exception of footnote 16, it is unclear as to exactly how much control is incessary. Partial ownership should be sufficient, but what if there is no ownership but common directors instead? Or what if the direct purchaser is a creditor or a debtor of the indirect purchaser?

There are as well a whole set of exceptions which may come under the heading of "vertical restraints." What if the manufacturers engaged in price fixing enforce their cartel in part through pricing restraints

---

[18] 431 U.S. 720, 736.

on their direct purchasers? In the Master Key litigation, the horizontal price fixing was enforced by vertical restraints on the price fixer's dealers.[19]

Cost plus contracts are another possible area of controversy. Although the Illinois Brick decision seemed to specify that only cost plus contracts where fixed quantities were specified would be excluded from the direct purchaser rule, the interpretation of such an exception may not be clear cut. In the more than 20 consolidated Cement and Concrete price fixing actions pending in the district court of Arizona, the defendants made a motion for summary dismissal on the basis of Illinois Brick since the plaintiffs were not direct purchasers from any of the defendants. Judge Muecke declined to dismiss the action precisely because at least four possible exceptions had not been ruled out. First, the defendants could have conspired with others from whom the plaintiffs are direct purchasers. Secondly the defendants could have owned or controlled an entity from which plaintiffs were direct purchasers. Further, there could have been a cost plus contract, or lastly there could have been a functional equivalent of a cost plus contract.[20]

It appears from all of this that there may be considerable unintended complexity of litigation as a result of Illinois Brick. In fact, if Illinois Brick holds, we may be merely substituting complex litigation on questions of ownership and control and the type of pricing rules utilized for litigation concerning the proof of passing on. The main alleged benefit of Illinois Brick as compared to some rule of recovery where indirect purchasers

---

[19] 1973-2 Trade Cases 74,680.

[20] ATRR, June 1, 1978.

may sue, is its administrative simplicity. But this so called administrative simplicity must be weighed against the new complexities that this decision is likely to introduce. However, it should be remembered that the questions concerning the two exceptions to the _Illinois Brick_ rule may be soon settled by definitive court rulings and thus the costs introduced by _Illinois Brick_ may be one time or lump sum costs. Still, no judicial or legislative rule can encompass all possibilities; thus, some continuing litigation costs concerning these exceptions are likely.

The costs of passing on, in contrast, are more likely to be recurrent costs which arise in all private antitrust litigation involving chains of distribution. Thus although the costs of apportioning damages among plaintiffs may be quite low, they are likely to arise in all chain of distribution cases, whereas the _Illinois Brick_ costs are apt to be mainly one time costs. A complete analysis of the benefits and costs of _Illinois Brick vis a vis_ its alternatives would in addition require a comparison of the deterrence and compensation aspects of the various rules, not just their administrative costs. It is here that a comparison of costs and benefits may strongly condemn _Illinois Brick_. While we have seen that this is true with respect to compensation we must await the conclusions of the next chapter to compare the deterrence aspects of _Illinois Brick_ and its alternatives.

To summarize the above discussion, we have seen that there are numerous criticisms dealing with the length, complexity, possible harassment, and manageability of antitrust actions. It would be a simple matter to conclude from this that _Illinois Brick_ is a welcome addition to the substantive body of private antitrust law since it prevents private actions from further deterioration in the domain of complexity. This conclusion was shown to be logically incorrect since it compares total costs and benefits rather than comparing the marginal benefits of deterrence and compensation with the marginal costs of the increased complexity of relaxing the Illinois Brick rule. Further, if our goal were to reduce the administrative costs of private antitrust enforcement, Illinois Brick would be both an arbitrary and ineffective instrument. All the above criticisms but one--the costs of proving passing on--are or could be addressed by proposals specifically designed to streamline private antitrust and class actions. It was shown that the one remaining potential problem--the necessity of having to prove passing on--may in fact be of manageable proportions. Further, this cost of proving passing on and the accompanying difficulties of multiparty litigation could be eliminated by at least one possible rule of recovery--that of the modified statute of limitations. The next section discusses the issue of multiple liability.

II. Multiple Liability

Multiple liability would theoretically be possible if Illinois Brick were overruled. This situation could arise if cases involving both direct and indirect purchasers allegedly injured by the same price fixer were pending in different courts or, less likely, at different times, and if the courts came to different conclusions on the question of passing on, and if these conclusions were both against the defendant.

Although multiple liability is theoretically possible, it is really an unimportant issue for several reasons. First, there are numerous procedures that can be invoked to avoid the possibility of multiple liability. Cases pending in different courts may be transferred and consolidated both for pre-trial procedures and for the purposes of trial. The newly created Judicial Panel on Multidistrict Litigation handles this goal of consolidation quite effectively and to this date about sixty clusters of antitrust cases have been consolidated under its authority. Once cases are consolidated, damages may be fairly allocated according to the specifications described in the Federal Rules of Civil Procedure.[21] In addition, the normal four year statute of limitations is exceeded by the length of many antitrust treble damage suits, therefore, it is quite unlikely that a potential plaintiff would wait for the completion of a previous case before filing.[22]

Secondly, the *occasional* or rare imposition of multiple liability should be preferred to *consistently* underdeterring potential antitrust violators. When a defendant's actions may have injured more than one class of plaintiffs, a rule should not be devised which in many cases will shield him from *all* liability in order to protect him from the rare event of *multiple* liability.

Finally, and perhaps most importantly, multiple liability *is* empirically inconsequential. According to Kenneth Reed, the Assistant Attorney General for Antitrust from the State of Arizona, "between 1968, the year of the *Hanover Shoe* decision, and 1977, when *Illinois Brick* came down, there has been no reported case in which a defendant has claimed that he was the victim of multiple liability."[23]

---

[21] See rule 42(a).

[22] Other procedures to prevent multiple liability from occurring are possible as well. Several are mentioned in the text of *In re Western Liquid Asphalt Cases*, 487 F. 2d 191, 201.

[23] *House Hearings*, p. 41.

Even if there were the increased prospect of multiple liability in the _future_ due perhaps in part to the tremendous increase in private litigation in general and class actions in particular, Illinois Brick would be too blunt an instrument to prevent multiple liability. If the modified statute of limitations scheme were implemented, no problem of multiple liability could exist. If other means were invoked to overturn Illinois Brick, easier means would be available to prevent the occurrence of multiple liability. For example legislation could oblige all parties in a chain of distribution to sue at the same time (in response perhaps to a notice or publication of the first suit) or else be barred by the findings of passing on as determined in the first suit.[24] The problem of multiple liability, then, is or could easily become inconsequential.

We stated earlier that there are three important criteria to be considered in choosing a rule of standing. They are (1) compensation, (2) the costs of enforcement, and (3) the deterrence of antitrust violators. The question of compensation or who is injured was addressed in Chapter III on incidence. The administrative cost issue as well as the multiple liability issue were just discussed in this chapter and we shall devote Chapter VI entirely to the question of deterrence, that is, who sues the price fixer. Before doing so, it will be useful to discuss a comparatively new and perhaps vitally important "event" in private antitrust enforcement, that of enforcement by the various states as purchasers of price fixed goods and as _parens patriae_. As we shall see, the pervasiveness and efficiency of private enforcement by the various state attorneys general may have an effect on the means chosen to overrule Illinois Brick.

---

[24] Phillip Areeda, House Hearings, p. 78.

III. State Attorneys General--The New Enforcers

There is considerable evidence that the state attorneys general have greatly increased their antitrust enforcement effects and expenditures in the past few years. This change is due to a number of factors the most important of which is probably the passage of the Hart-Scott-Rodino Antitrust Improvements Act of 1976 which coupled with other legislation provided for monetary and other kinds of aid to the various state antitrust departments. More recently the Illinois Brick decision itself has had an important effect on state enforcement simply because more than 90% of state purchases are indirect. This section begins by describing the effect of the Antitrust Improvements Act and of Illinois Brick on state enforcement, and ends with a discussion of the effects of state enforcement on the various possible alternatives to overrule the Illinois Brick decision.

The overall scope of state antitrust enforcement is quite large. In a speech to a Federal Bar Association Conference, Chauncey Browning, the chairman of the Antitrust Committee of the National Association of Attorneys General, said that by conservative estimates the states had pending lawsuits of $200 million as indirect purchasers alone.[25] The state of California alone recovered over $44 million over the period of 1973-77, primarily in the antibiotics, snack foods, gypsum and asphalt industries.[26] One of the most successful private antitrust suits ever brought (in terms of the magnitude of damages recovered), the Western Liquid Asphalt Cases, was initiated by the states who recovered $30 million with no assistance from the Department of

---

[25] ATRR, Nov. 10, 1977.

[26] Michael Spiegel, Assistant Attorney General, California, Senate Hearings, p. 125.

Justice.[27]

At the same time Congress passed the Hart-Scott-Rodino Bill, it authorized $30 million in separate legislation to improve the antitrust enforcement capabilities of the states.[28] This legislation provided for $10 million a year for three years to be disbursed as subsidies to the state attorneys general's offices to further or in some cases begin antitrust enforcement. Initial disbursements were made during the fall of 1977 ranging in size from $123,000 to $412,000 to the various states. For as many as 25 states the federal funding meant the creation of a two or three attorney antitrust office for the first time. For those states with antitrust departments already in existence, the funding usually served to increase their staffing, but in some cases served also to purchase and/or maintain computer services for functions such as detecting bid rigging to state and local government. In order to insure that enforcement would increase, rather than simply changing its source of funding, the legislation required that these grants to the states could not be used to supplant state funds. Indeed state enforcement did grow. At least according to the grant proposals, the number of state attorneys employed in antitrust enforcement were to more than double from 92 to 195 as a result of the federal funding.[29]

Since the grants were intended to last only three years, the states

---

[27] Spiegal, Senate Hearings, p. 109.

[28] ATRR, Sept. 15, 1977, and Legal Times of Washington, Nov. 27, 1978, p. 15. This grant program was attached to the 1976 extension of the Law Enforcement Assistance Administration.

[29] ATRR, Sept. 15, 1977.

have been counseled to use the funding to begin programs which would be self sustaining after the money has run out. Some states are doing exactly that. As of December 1977, ten states including California, Connecticut, Massachusetts, New Jersey, and Ohio, had antitrust revolving funds.[30] A revolving fund is essentially a "bank account" usually in the custody of the state treasurer in which is deposited all or part of the funds awarded to the state for recovery of costs and fees in antitrust actions. Such funds can be used at the discretion of the attorney general for the payment of all costs and expenses incurred in enforcing the (federal and state) antitrust laws. Thus, this revolving fund gives state enforcers significant incentives to bring the most important suits (at least in terms of the value of their recovery).[31] These incentives were seen to be lacking at the U.S. Department of Justice! The state enforcement bureau is compensated then, not in publicity in proportion to the number of cases it has won regardless of their significance, but rather is rewarded by its ability to grow larger and more important--in direct proportion to the monetary value of its recoveries. Indeed, particularly when federal funding runs out, the stick as well as the carrot may well provide powerful incentives to encourage vigorous enforcement of the antitrust laws.

In addition to providing monetary incentives in the form of grants to states, Congress has also legislated in the new Antitrust Improvements Act of 1976 that information about possible antitrust actions be readily

---

[30] Telephone conversation with Lynne Ross, special assistant to the Chairman, National Association of Attorneys General, July 1978.

[31] It is the agency and not the enforcer who is actually being compensated. Therefore, this conclusion assumes that the decision-makers in the state agencies desire growth for its own sake.

made available to the state attorneys general by the Attorney General of the United States. The Act provides in part that,

> To assist a state attorney general...in bringing any action under this act, the Attorney General of the United States shall...make available to him, to the extent permitted by law, any investigative files or other materials which are or may be relevant or material....[32]

"To the extent permitted by law" has already been interpreted very broadly by the courts. In July of 1977 the Department of Justice agreed with the state of Maryland, who brought one of the first parens patriae actions, to allow Maryland immediate access to Grand Jury documents and transcripts relating to the pending real estate commission price fixing case.[33] This disclosure was upheld by the U.S. District Court in agreeing that the amended Clayton Act constituted a valid exception to the usual rule of grand jury secrecy.[34]

Thus far we have seen some of the positive effects of the recent Antitrust Improvements Act on the ability and willingness of state authorities to help enforce the antitrust laws. Perhaps an even more pervasive effect on state enforcement has been as a result of the Illinois Brick decision itself. As indicated above, at least 90% of state purchases of goods and services are as indirect purchasers. Unless the states are willing to expend their energies litigating the exceptions to the Illinois Brick rule and other novel legal theories, over 90% of their potential cases are swept away by this decision. On the other hand, it can be argued

---

[32] Clayton §4F(b) as amended in 1976.

[33] ATRR, July 14, 1977.

[34] ATRR, June 8, 1978.

that the states are on the whole probably more resourceful as a result of Illinois Brick. Since the preponderance of state purchases are indirect, the states have devised an innovative, although far from foolproof, way of getting around the Illinois Brick rule. Several states have begun to ask contractors to assign to the state their rights to sue antitrust violators for treble damages. The National Association of Attorneys General has been coordinating an effort to have all state purchasing agents seek assignment clauses in contracts. An NAAG subcommittee has even drafted a model contract clause for possible use by all the states.[35]

Despite the obvious appeal of such a simple solution to effectively allow the states to circumvent the Illinois Brick rule, the "assignment" of the right to sue to states has many drawbacks. First, individual purchasing agents may have little incentive to seek such clauses unless forced to do so. Likewise, contractors may be reluctant to do so since they could be subject to discovery by two of the parties they would least like to know about their business--their customers and suppliers. Most importantly assignment of the right to sue would be considerably more difficult, if not impossible, if there were another layer of indirect purchasers intervening between the direct purchaser and the state. Still, obtaining assignment of the right to sue represents a considerable improvement over the outright exclusion of all indirect purchaser suits.

Some states have also demonstrated considerable ingenuity in altering their state antitrust laws to circumvent the Illinois Brick rule against indirect purchaser suits. Most states have "Little Sherman Acts" and "Little Clayton Acts" which have been used increasingly frequently in recent

---

[35] ATRR, Oct. 13, 1977.

years. Many of these state laws are near replicas of the respective Federal Sherman or Clayton Acts. In addition, at least several include the provision that where the interpretation of these acts is in doubt, the corresponding interpretation provided by the federal courts is to be binding.[36] In other words, the announcement of the Illinois Brick decision by the Supreme Court to interpret the Clayton Act had at the same time a tremendous effect on the interpretation of the state antitrust laws of various states. In direct response to the Illinois Brick decision, several states have moved to amend their state antitrust laws to allow indirect purchasers to sue and collect treble damages. However, while it would be nice to think that all indirect purchaser suits could be potentially handled under the state laws, this would not be the case. While the state laws may be adequate substitutes for federal law in some instances, the handling of multidistrict cases would be in doubt. Whereas under federal law some of the largest and most important cases are brought by large clusters of states and other parties which are consolidated for the purposes of pretrial hearings and for trial in a single district, such an approach would not be possible for states suing as indirect purchasers under their own state laws. The benefits of the consolidation of cases, both in terms of conserving the resources of otherwise duplicated effort and of the increased deterrence provided by these otherwise improbable suits, are immense and would be lost if the states could not sue jointly under federal law. Therefore, despite the ingenuity of the states in taking actions such as seeking assignments and amending their state statutes to allow direct

---

[36] California, Arizona, and Missouri are three examples, telephone conversations with their respective Antitrust Directors, 9/28/78, 10/2/78, and 9/29/78.

purchasers to sue, Illinois Brick, if it is allowed to remain law, will have tremendously deleterious effects on the ability of the states to help enforce the antitrust laws.

The states have clearly emerged as important actors in the overall enforcement of the antitrust laws. The advent of Illinois Brick has all but reduced their role to potential actors in enforcing the antitrust laws. The following paragraphs shall seek to demonstrate that the states should be allowed to sue and recover treble damages from guilty parties even when they or the citizens of their states are indirect purchasers. State enforcement, especially under the new parens patriae provisions, provides distinct advantages over other private enforcement and at the same time does not suffer many of the problems of complexity and unmanageability that concern the proponents of Illinois Brick. An examination of these differences would be in order.

State vs. "Other" Private Enforcement

There are several important reasons why the states may be more effective enforcers than other private parties. Here are a few of those reasons.

(1) Harassment--States are far less likely than are private firms to harass other firms by bringing groundless antitrust suits. This tendency is reinforced by the parens patriae provision that the court may award a reasonable attorney's fee to a prevailing defendant upon a finding that the state has acted "in bad faith" or "for oppressive reasons."[37] Further, to the extent that it is lawyers who solicit clients to harass

---

[37] One might be tempted to argue that states may bring cases against firms for political reasons. This too would presumably be discouraged under the provisions for parens patriae.

other firms by bringing unmeritorious suits, state enforcement will completely eliminate this problem.

(2) _Costs of Suit_--Again under the _parens patriae_ provisions of the Antitrust Improvements Act, states have two clear advantages over ordinary plaintiffs. Notice may be given by publication, rather than by the far more costly individual mailings, and aggregate damages may be computed by statistical sampling methods rather than by costly individual computations. There may be savings in non-parens suits as well. The purchases of the state governments and its jurisdictions are often quite large. Therefore, the average costs of state suits (that is, costs as a proportion of total recovery) are likely to be much lower, particularly when in-house attorneys are utilized. In addition, the states can make use of their large purchases of a wide variety of products to utilize a computer to help detect bid rigging--something individual firms cannot do. The states are also in a position to (and do) cooperate with each other in bringing cases. Such cooperation may further conserve resources by avoiding the duplication of effort.

(3) _Information_--States may receive liberal help from the Department of Justice in the form of valuable information pertaining to potential and ongoing cases which may include, as we have seen above, Grand Jury documents. These sources of information are obviously not available to private parties.

(4) _Manageability_--Multiparty litigation is viewed by many as inordinately complex and unnecessarily costly. However, adding the state enforcers even as indirect purchasers to the list of plaintiffs who have a right to sue for treble damages would do very little to reduce the manageability of complex cases but would go a long way toward improving

other aspects of enforcement such as deterrence.

(5) <u>Deterrence</u>--Adding any party or parties to the list of allowable plaintiffs will always add to the deterrence of antitrust violators (unless of course it correspondingly <u>reduces</u> the willingness or ability of other parties to sue). This proposition is even more true with respect to state enforcers since they can be expected to act in the public interest and provide a safety valve for private enforcement. Considerable evidence will be presented in the next chapter to bolster this view. At this point it will be instructive to mention a single example. In the very sizable <u>Petroleum Products</u> litigation pending on the west coast, the only parties to have filed suit are seven states (and one city)![38]

Conclusion

We have seen that three major sets of issues required our attention in order to decide between the available alternatives for overruling <u>Illinois Brick</u>. The issues relating to compensation were discussed in Chapter III, the related issues of administrative costs and of multiple liability were discussed in this chapter and the issues relating to deterrence will be handled in the next.

We have seen that although there are problems of complexity and manageability inherent in private antitrust enforcement, most of these problems could be greatly alleviated by the institution of procedureal reforms to govern class actions. The one problem that cannot easily be

---

[38] <u>In re Petroleum Products Antitrust Litigation</u>, MDL 150, telephone conversation with Kirk Johns, Office of the Attorney General, Oregon, 10/4/78.

handled by procedural reforms is that of the cost of proving passing on. However, we have seen that the costs of apportioning damages between competing plaintiffs can be quite low in instances where the issue of total liability has already been settled. Further, the modified statute of limitations plan (and perhaps other plans as well) avoids all of these difficulties. Even if reforms intended to alleviate the costs and complexities of antitrust litigation were not made immediately, adding fifty states (as indirect purchasers) to the list of possible plaintiffs in antitrust cases would do little to reduce the manageability of antitrust cases, but would go a long way toward more effective enforcement and would of course satisfy the intent of Congress in passing the <u>parens patriae</u> title of the Hart-Scott-Rodino Act.

Multiple liability, while theoretically possible, is empirically inconsequential and therefore should not be a major determining factor in developing a rule of standing for indirect purchasers. Even if it were empirically meaningful, it is expressly excluded by the <u>parens patriae</u> provisions and could be excluded by appropriate legislation for the states' own recoveries as well. Therefore, adding the fifty states as allowable plaintiffs, even as indirect purchasers, would not appreciably alter the possibility of multiple liability.

In the vast majority of cases it is not the direct purchaser who is injured, but rather the final consumer. This of course applies to states both in their proprietary capacities and as <u>parens patriae</u>. Therefore, the addition of states as allowable indirect purchaser plaintiffs would serve the compensatory purposes of effective antitrust enforcement.

It remains to be seen whether direct or indirect purchasers are the most active enforcers. It will be shown, however, that there are many instances where direct purchasers have for one reason or another not sued their suppliers. The states on the other hand, have no reason to hold back from suing, and in fact have been very active enforcers. They have been the beneficiaries of some of the largest recoveries in history, and in doing so have provided a valuable safety valve for private enforcement.

Thus it appears that at a very minimum the states should be allowed to sue, both as <u>parens patriae</u> and as purchasers of their own goods and services, even when they are indirect purchasers! Whether this liberalization should be enlarged to include all potential private enforcers will await results of the next chapter on direct purchaser enforcement.

CHAPTER VI

WHO SUES THE PRICE FIXER?

We have previously determined that there are three distinct goals to be considered in deciding on rules of standing in private treble damage cases. These goals are (1) the deterrence of antitrust violators, (2) the compensation of its victims, and (3) the minimization of the administrative costs of enforcement. In Chapter II above deterrence and the minimization of enforcement costs were grouped together under the heading of the efficiency of antitrust enforcement. In that chapter a model was developed in which efficient enforcement was defined as the minimization of the sum of two costs: (1) the welfare losses due to undeterred violations, and (2) the costs of enforcement by all parties concerned.

In order to determine the best way to overrule the Illinois Brick decision, we must assess the available alternatives with respect to their ability to achieve each of the above goals. The compensation issue was handled in Chapter III. We first developed a partial equilibrium model indicating how much of the initial overcharge is borne by the respective parties in a chain of manufacturing or distribution under varying market structure, cost, and demand conditions. We then applied this model to a sample of recent price fixing cases to conclude that the indirect purchaser usually bears the overcharge burden, especially in the long run.

The administrative cost issue was similarly handled in Chapter V. In that chapter we indicated that there may be an increased cost of proving passing on if _Illinois Brick_ were overruled by Congress, but this cost must be weighed against the possible increases in costs due to the complexities brought about by the _Illinois Brick_ decision itself. If instead a modified statute of limitations scheme were utilized to overrule _Illinois Brick_, there would be virtually no additional administrative costs of enforcement. The remaining determination which must be made concerns the deterrence issue. Are direct or indirect purchasers more likely to better enforce the antitrust laws? This is the central question to be addressed in this chapter. Then the assessments of deterrence, compensation, and the costs of enforcement can be weighed and balanced to determine the best way to overrule the _Illinois Brick_ decision.

It should first be mentioned that the degree of deterrence of antitrust violators cannot be equated with the number or the frequency of antitrust suits. It is impossible to determine how many antitrust suits actually filed of any given size are necessary for a certain degree of deterrence. Rather deterrence is a function of potential violators perceptions of the willingness and ability of potential plaintiffs to detect a violation, file suit and receive a recovery, and on the extent of penalities. In the terminology of Chapter II, depending on the position of the violation curve we could have a low level of antitrust suits consistent with very few violations, and a high level of antitrust suits consistent with a considerably higher number of antitrust violations. Thus, by observing the total number of direct purchaser treble damage suits, we can infer little or nothing about the extent to which antitrust violators are deterred. We can, however, observe the _relative_ frequencies of direct and indirect

```
Number of
Violations |
                              S(V,k,L)
                        
                         V₂(S,k,L)
                       V₁(S,k,L)
                                    Number of
                                    Suits
```

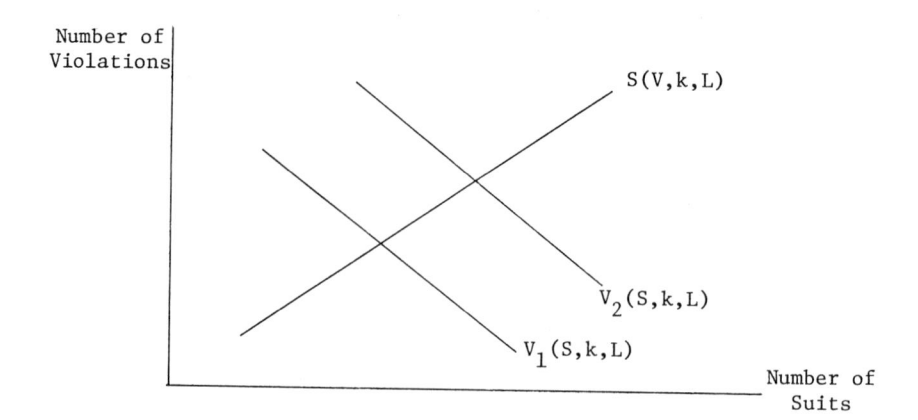

FIGURE 1. Deterrence Cannot be Inferred from Number of Suits

purchaser suits. A comparison of the relative frequencies of suits brought by these two kinds of plaintiffs would give us a good idea of their _relative_ contribution to the deterrence of antitrust violators.

This chapter seeks to determine whether direct or indirect purchasers (or both) can best enforce the antitrust laws. There is considerable "casual evidence" that in many instances direct purchasers do not sue their suppliers. This evidence is the subject of the first section. Following this, a more systematic approach is explored to determine whether in fact the casual evidence presented in the first section concerning who sues the price fixer withstands further empirical investigation. The second section explains a case by case approach which uses regression analysis to make this determination. While interesting, this approach is shown to produce too many serious biases to be reliable. In the third section a second approach is attempted. The fifty state attorneys general are surveyed to determine whether in the litigations in which they were involved, direct purchasers were active, and whether their behavior changed as a reaction to the Illinois Brick decision. The fourth and final section of this chapter will analyze the results of this survey and make conclusions.

I. Who Sues the Price Fixer?--Casual Evidence

In this section it will be shown that there have been many instances where direct purchasers were for one reason or another reluctant to sue their suppliers. Several possible explanations are offered to make sense of these observations. This is followed by a brief description of studies conducted by others concerning the very same question--the willingness of direct purchasers to sue their suppliers. Unfortunately, since their results are inconsistent and their methodology subject to bias, no confident conclusions can be made. A further attempt to obtain a more comprehensive view and to avoid the pitfalls of these studies is made in the next section. We now turn to evidence of particular instances where direct purchasers did not sue their suppliers.

1) In re Western Liquid Asphalt Cases. In the Western Liquid Asphalt Cases[1] state governments led by the state of California who were indirect purchasers of asphalt, sued and received about $30 million from the defendant producers of asphalt. At the same time virtually none of the contractors who purchased asphalt directly from the defendants and resold to the plaintiffs ever came forward to challenge the violations. The court maintained,

> Counsel at oral argument pointed out that only one contractor in California, and three in Oregon, have sued appellants--a very small percentage of

---

[1] 487 F. 2d 191 (9th Cir. 1973).

> those involved. No contractors have sued in the
> states of Arizona, Alaska and Washington. It is
> most likely that the four year statute of limita-
> tions...has run on those who have not sued.[2]

A better perspective on the true miniscule magnitude of the proportion of the direct purchasers who did sue is more obvious when one realizes that price fixed asphalt was purchased in 37,000 <u>different</u> <u>contracts</u> with the price fixers.[3]

It should be noted that the direct purchasers were found to use a cost plus percentage markup pricing system. Thus, given the probable inelasticity of the demand for their product,[4] the defendant's price fixing was probably profitable to them. Also, documents obtained from the defendants indicated that they controlled a high percentage of their direct customers of asphalt, either through stock ownership or through credit arrangement. Had <u>Illinois Brick</u> been law at the time of the <u>Western</u>

---

[2] 487 F. 2d at 198.

[3] Ibid.

[4] The elasticity of demand for liquid asphalt, the price fixer's product, is a derived demand, derived from the demand for the roads for which the liquid asphalt is an input. The elasticity of derived demand, η_d, is related to the elasticity of final product demand, η_p, in the following way:

$$\eta_D = \sigma + k\eta_p, \text{ where } \eta > 0,$$

where σ is the elasticity of substitution between the price fixed input and the other input in a two factor production function, and k is the factor share to the price fixed input, $f_1 x_1/Q$. The equation above has assumed that the substitute input is perfectly elastically supplied. See George Stigler, <u>A Theory of Price</u> (New York: Macmillan, 1966), p. 346. Thus, since σ in this case can be expected to be close to zero, and k, the factor share to asphalt, and η_p the elasticity of demand for roads, to be low, the derived demand for asphalt should also be very low.

Liquid Asphalt Cases, and if footnote 16 of Illinois Brick (the ownership or control exception) and the cost plus exception had been interpreted literally or even strictly, the vast majority of plaintiffs in Western Liquid Asphalt would have been denied recovery.

2) Cement and Concrete Antitrust Litigation[5]--Four states who purchased cement or concrete from contractors or ready-mix suppliers were active in a case consolidated for trial in Arizona. According to Robert Hill, the assistant attorney general from Colorado, one of the states involved, no ready-mix suppliers had filed suit against the defendant. Again according to Hill the suit was the largest potential damage case in existence on behalf of state governments.[6] Immediately after Illinois Brick was decided, the states were served with requests by the defendants, asking if they had been direct purchasers, in order to dismiss the litigation. As we have seen above, the case was not dismissed immediately but is pending until a determination can be made as to whether any of the exceptions to the Illinois Brick rule apply. The pricing system used by the direct purchasers is undoubtably cost plus and the elasticity of demand very low. Thus, it is probable that the direct purchasers actually profited from the violation.

3) Antibiotics--In the antibiotics litigation which was comprised of 166 separate cases against the defendant antibiotics manufacturers, a global settlement was made between the manufacturers and a large portion of the plaintiffs' classes. In this court approved settlement, described

---

[5] In re Cement and Concrete Antitrust Litigation, Master File Civ. No. 76-408-A PHX CAM (D. Ariz.).

[6] Senate Hearings, p. 106.

in West Virginia v. Chas. Pfizer & Co.,[7] the notice of a settlement fund was distributed to 55,000 drug wholesalers and retailers. Of this total only 4,100 claims were filed although the money was very easily available. 1,500 wholesalers and retailers expressly excluded themselves from the class with letters expressing indignation. One letter reprinted in part in the opinion reads as follows:

> Any pharmacy claiming damages is, in my opinion, guilty of lying. All pharmacies base their retail prices for drugs on their costs, either using a fixed percentage or a professional fee. Either way, they do not suffer damages due to higher wholesale costs of these drugs. If anyone has a complaint, it would be the individual consumer, not the pharmacists.[8]

The demand for antibiotics is undoubtably highly inelastic. The pricing system is undeniably cost plus in nature, although without specifying a fixed quantity and therefore probably not within the reach of the exception to Illinois Brick.

> According to affidavits of experts in the field, the overwhelming majority of drug stores in the period 1953-1966 charged a uniform markup of 66 2/3% over cost. If so, this would mean that any overcharge by defendants in violation of the antitrust laws was passed on to the end use purchaser. The result is that wholesalers and retailers, far from sustaining damages, made substantial profits from any antitrust violations.[9]

4) Beef[10]--165 beef producers were consolidated in the Northern

---

[7] 314 F. Supp. 710.

[8] 314 F. Supp. at 746.

[9] 314 F. Supp. at 745.

[10] In re Beef Industry Antitrust Litigation, MDL 248.

District of Texas for the purposes of suing more than 25 retail food stores and chains for price fixing and monopolization. The defendants were charged with price fixing by using their monopsony power to hold down the price of beef to packers, the direct sellers. This artificially low monopsony price was allegedly transmitted backwards to the plaintiff beef producers and feeders. As a result of Illinois Brick, Judge Taylor dismissed all the actions of plaintiffs and no one else was suing.[11] According to some of the plaintiffs, the packers did not want to disturb their relationships with their customers, the retail food stores and chains, and hence did not sue for damages.

5) Plumbing Fixtures[12]--In the plumbing fixtures cases the counsel of plaintiff found it common for wholesalers or plumbing contractors either to refuse to join suits against the defendants or to express hesitancy about doing so for fear of disturbing business relationships with its suppliers.[13] An attorney for one of the plaintiffs stated that he "received several calls from members of the various alleged classes of plaintiffs...asking about the nature of the litigation and concluding that the risks to their relationships with their suppliers did not warrant joining the fray."[14] Although there is no available evidence on the pricing rules of plumbing fixtures wholesalers or contractors, since sinks, tubs, and toilets comprise such a small component of the final product--housing (and

---

[11] ATRR, Nov. 3, 1977 and April 20, 1978.

[12] Multidistrict Private Civil Treble Damage Litigation Involving Plumbing Fixtures, MDL 3.

[13] Wheeler, pp. 1331-1332.

[14] Wheeler, p. 1332 (footnote).

since these items are not frequently purchased alone), the derived elasticity of demand is undoubtably quite small. It may well be that the conspiracy was profitable to the direct purchasers.

6) <u>Dairy Products</u>--According to Kenneth Reed, the Assistant Attorney General for antitrust in Arizona, in a recent Arizona suit against the dairy industry, more than half of the grocery stores "opted out" of the class. He surmised from this that these grocers may have participated--and profited--from the conspiracy.[15]

7) <u>Wheelchairs</u>--Private treble damage actions seeking damages for overcharges due to the monopolization of wheelchairs by Everest Jenings were filed by indirect purchasers of wheelchairs in response to a government indictment of the defendant for monopolization. The single independent distributor failed to bring suit even after <u>Illinois Brick</u>, probably due to either its sharing in the profitability of the monopolization or fear of losing its distributorship.[16]

It should be noted that <u>all</u> of the above examples possess one or more of the following characteristics: a cost plus pricing system, very low elasticity of demand, or there is a relationship of ownership or control by the manufacturer where the direct purchaser is afraid of retaliation.

In addition to this casual evidence of particular examples of situations where direct purchasers have not sued their suppliers, there is testimony that these examples are not unique. Josef Cooper, plaintiff's

---

[15] ATRR, April 20, 1978.

[16] Statement of Josef Cooper, Chairman of the Private Litigation Committee of the ABA Antitrust Section, <u>House Hearings</u>, pp. 171-172.

attorney and chairman of the Private Litigation Committee of the ABA Antitrust Section, testified to the Senate subcommittee that, "I have personally counseled numerous potential plaintiffs who have elected not to proceed with litigation because of possible disruption to their business or possible termination of existing sources of supply or services."[17]

There are also various "studies" available attempting to determine whether direct or indirect purchasers play a more active role in private antitrust enforcement. Handler and Blechman made a pilot study of the antitrust cases pending in the Southern District of New York. Of the 69 cases brought by buyers or sellers only 3 were brought by indirect purchasers"[18] Although this result seems startling, the study is flawed for at least two reasons. First, the sample includes cases where there is no chain of distribution. Where price fixing takes place at the retail level it is not surprising to find that if a case is filed at all, it is filed by a direct purchaser. The sample may also have been biased for yet a more important reason. The second circuit in which the southern District of New York is located, had held (before Illinois Brick) that indirect purchasers could not recover for overcharges. In an atmosphere so inhospitable to indirect purchaser suits, it is not surprising that indirect purchasers did not file frequently.

Another study was conducted by David Berger of Berger and Montague, Philadelphia, who concluded that indirect purchasers have played "a significant role in private enforcement." Berger surveyed 57 class actions brought since 1960 and found that 60% involved both indirect and direct

---

[17] House Hearings, p. 171.

[18] ATRR, April 13, 1978.

purchasers while 25% involved indirect purchasers only.[19]

It is clear from this evidence that there are numerous instances where the direct purchaser does not sue his supplier. It is also clear that any generalization from these few examples to conclusions about the activity or inactivity of direct purchasers suing their suppliers would be hazardous. The two studies cited above came to opposite conclusions. Neither of these studies will be examined further because they both introduce serious biases. It will be shown in the next section that these studies and indeed any case by case study cannot be relied on to give an accurate answer to the question of who is best able to enforce the antitrust laws because of the important biases they inevitably include.

II. Case by Case Approach

One possible method of determining who sues the price fixer would be to observe from a cross sectional sample of cases brought during a relatively short time period, the identities (direct or indirect purchasers) of plaintiffs who bring suit and receive recoveries in treble damage actions. By taking a representative set of cases one should be able to determine two things. First, it should be possible to observe the identities of active plaintiffs and thus their relative contribution to the deterrence of antitrust violators. Secondly, it should also be possible to identify the market characteristics which influence the willingness of direct or indirect purchasers to sue antitrust violators.

The first determination--the relative contribution to deterrence of

---

[19] ATRR, February 23, 1978.

direct and indirect purchasers--can be easily seen in the aggregate by simply adding up cases brought by the two classes of plaintifss and comparing numbers. Provided that the sample is representative and that the two classes of parties are equally diligent in their litigation and in fact extract treble damages with equal probabilities, a comparison of cases brought by direct and indirect purchasers would give a clear indication of their relative contribution to the deterrence of antitrust violators.

The second determination--the conditions under which direct and indirect purchasers are likely to sue the antitrust violators--requires the use of multiple regression. A regression approach would indicate the relative contribution of the various parties to antitrust deterrence under <u>particular</u> circumstances, such as when demand is inelastic or when there exist significant credit arrangements between direct purchasers and their suppliers.

A regression could be run with a dichotomous left hand side variable (direct purchasers sue, don't sue), and whose independent variables include those many factors hypothesized likely to affect a direct purchaser's willingness and ability to sue his supplier. One possible factor would be the elasticity of (derived) demand for the price fixed product (as a proxy for the extent of pass on). Another would be some measure(s) of the existence of potential <u>control</u> over the direct purchaser by the price fixer. Three possible proxies for control could be included. These are the presence or absence of partial stock ownership, the extension of credit, and the existence of shortages in the industry. A third potentially important variable might be the size of the direct purchaser(s) in order to determine if there is a size threshold below which active litigation is unlikely. Another candidate might be some element of the market structure of the direct purchaser class, perhaps either concentration or the number of firms, for a number of distinct reasons. The concentration of a market, for example, may affect the extent of passing on, and therefore the extent of injury to various parties. It may drastically affect the costs of suit for the individual firm. In addition, price fixers may be perceived to be less likely to "retaliate" against a whole class of plaintiffs than a single plaintiff. A final possible determinant might be whether or not the indirect purchaser had brought suit.[20] A similar regression could be run for indirect purchaser suits. A possible linear specification of the suggested direct purchaser regression would be as follows:

$$SUE = \beta_0 + \beta_1 ELASTICITY + \beta_2 OWNERSHIP + \beta_3 CREDIT + \beta_4 SHORTAGE + \beta_5 SALES + \beta_6 CONCENTRATION + \beta_7 IPSUIT^{[21]} + \epsilon .$$

These regression coefficients would predict <u>probabilities</u> of direct (or indirect) purchaser suits given the particular characteristics of the product and the direct (or indirect) purchaser class. When all the independent variables take on their mean values the constant term gives the average propensity to sue from the aggregate sample. The individual regression coefficients would indicate the extent to which the probability of suit is influenced by various changes in the characteristics of the

---

[20] This variable may not be truly exogenous. Indirect purchasers in some instances may sue in <u>response</u> to direct purchaser suits. It is also conceivable that indirect purchasers may sue because direct purchasers are <u>not</u> suing. Although the direction and extent of bias is unclear, due to the endogeneity of this variable, it may not be an appropriate right hand side variable.

[21] See previous footnote.

product or market. If for example, β_1 for direct purchasers were positive and significant, and β_1 for indirect purchasers were negative and significant, this would indicate that the elasticity of demand significantly affected both parties' willingness or ability to sue and in opposite directions. One might conclude that to some extent the propensity to sue is specialized in either the direct or indirect purchaser class according to elasticity. Such information might be useful in indicating the relative deterrence value of direct and indirect purchasers under varying market elasticities, and therefore the probable conditions under which a direct purchaser rule would be adequate to deter antitrust violators. It would also shed light on the conditions under which deterrence would suffer due to the presence of only direct purchasers as plaintiffs. Here exceptions to the Illinois Brick rule may be in order.

Unfortunately, there would be tremendous conceptual and empirical problems with such an approach. First the data are almost impossible to obtain. Further, even if perfect data were available, the results would be biased and inconclusive. The following paragraphs lay out both the conceptual and the empirical problems with such a cross sectional case analysis approach.

(1) **Large numbers of cases**--There have been an astounding number of treble damage cases filed since 1968, the date of the Hanover Shoe decision. The administrative office of the U.S. courts reports that the number filed in the last four years alone exceeds 5,000,[22] a very high proportion of which allege price fixing. Therefore any research on a

---

[22] Annual Report, Administrative Office of the U.S. Courts, 1976, p. 191.

case by case basis would necessarily involve sampling of some form or another. The next several sections lay out the reasons why sampling would be biased and inconclusive. As we shall see these biases would occur whether the sampling is done on cases filed or opinions issued.

(2) Settlements--An unknown but probably very high proportion of antitrust suits are settled out of court. With few exceptions written opinions are not available for these cases. Indeed, it may well be company policy to keep such settlements a secret. Thus even if one were to obtain opinions of all antitrust cases filed, they would be missing the vital segment of settled cases.

(3) Difficulty of Determining the Identities and Characteristics of Plaintiffs--Even if one decided that the absence of settled cases did not seriously bias the results of a case by case approach, the written opinions which are available are often of little assistance in determining the identities of active plaintiffs. Many written opinions concern themselves with peripheral issues only and provide little clue to whether the purchasers are direct or indirect. The names of the vast majority of the parties in large class actions are not available since most of these are listed as John Doe et al. v. .... In many instances the number of individual plaintiffs total in the thousands.[23] In order to obtain the necessary documents to clarify the identities of these parties, one would have to obtain them from the ninety-four individual district courts in the U.S.

(4) Suits Filed vs. Active Litigants--Even if one were to determine which parties filed suit in each "case," the results might still be

---

[23] See for example, In re Plumbing Fixtures Antitrust Litigation where at least 370 separate suits, many or most of which were brought as class actions, were coordinated and consolidated for pretrial proceedings in the Eastern District of Pennsylvania, 342 F. Supp. 756.

ambiguous and inconclusive. This is true simply because the mere act of filing an antitrust treble damage claim is not equivalent to active and aggressive participation in a case from the standpoint of effective antitrust deterrence. One can well imagine cases where in a very large nationwide price fixing conspiracy, one or two insignificant plaintiffs file suit on behalf of a nationwide class of large corporations. The small plaintiffs may even be "solicited" by attorneys seeking large contingency fees. If the individual plaintiffs have only a small monetary interest in the litigation, they may be likely to settle for small sums. This is particularly true in settled cases where the lawyer for the class may be tempted to offer to settle with the defendant for a small judgment and a large attorney's fee. This arrangement is favorable to all parties involved except the plaintiffs whose individual members have only a small interest in the litigation.[24] In such instances, the presence of plaintiffs, direct purchasers or otherwise, should not be taken to be synonymous with the deterrence of antitrust violators since the payoffs are so small. Evidence of such occurrences will be presented later in this chapter. From the perspective of deterrence, such instances are conceptually similar to:

(5) *Harassment Suits*--If treble damage actions are filed by unmeritorious plaintiffs hoping for a quick settlement, such suits would not be effective deterrents to antitrust violations. Therefore, the inability to distinguish between meritorious litigants and undeserving plaintiffs who would be willing to settle for only a small fraction of alleged treble

---

[24]It is of course true that judges must approve the settlement agreement. However, as Richard Posner points out, it is the lawyers who control the judge's access to the requisite information about the extent of damages as well as the attorney's work on the case. See Richard Posner, *Economic Analysis of the Law* (Boston: Little Brown and Company, 1972), pp. 346-351.

damages would bias any results obtained.

While the above paragraphs indicated problems and biases resulting from the incompleteness, inaccuracy, or misleading nature of data, the following paragraphs demonstrate why even perfect data would not produce accurate or even tolerable results.

(6) The <u>Illinois Brick Objection</u>--The <u>Illinois Brick</u> opinion reasons that the concentration of the ability to sue in the direct purchaser class would improve its likelihood of suit. This might be true both because the direct purchaser would not have to contend with the costly proof of passing on and also because he would not be faced with the prospect of sharing his recovery with one or more indirect purchasers. As we are, in part, testing the empirical validity of the Supreme Court's reasoning, we must not assume it away. Direct purchasers may not have filed suit in the 1968-1977 era due simply to the prospect of having to share recovery or prove passing on, while an <u>Illinois Brick</u> rule might have produced the opposite response. Thus, any result obtained on direct purchaser suits would clearly be biased downward although by an unknown magnitude.

(7) <u>Indirect Purchaser Biases</u>--The reasoning applied to direct purchasers above applies with equal force to indirect purchaser plaintiffs. Indirect purchasers may be more willing to sue if they do not have to contend with either the costly proof of passing-on or the possibility of having to share part of their recovery with the direct purchasers. This would be the case, for example, with the modified statute of limitations scheme explained above. Thus, indirect purchaser suits observed from empirical data would likely be much lower than the actual number of suits observed in the modified statute of limitations world.

A far more important reason exists, however, to account for a severe downward bias in any empirically derived results of indirect purchaser suits. Indirect purchasers may not have sued because their circuit may have ruled that indirect purchasers did not have standing to sue. In the plumbing fixtures case where overcharges on sinks, toilets, and tubs were alleged to have been incorporated in the price of housing, the court stated that it "strikes the court as incredible"...."if the price of a house were determined not by the shifts in the supply and demand in the market for homes as a whole but rather"....by overcharges on small items.[25] The court apparently did not understand the relationship between cost and supply and thereby denied standing to builders and owners of houses. There would be no reason for an indirect purchaser plaintiff to file a treble damage suit in a circuit where the court had already ruled that it does not have standing. Such rulings were often based on Hanover Shoe, and articulated reasoning not dissimilar to that underlying the Illinois Brick opinion. Where the circuits had not ruled, the potential implications of the Hanover Shoe decision may have scared away potential indirect purchaser plaintiffs. It should be mentioned that there were circuits where the Appeals Court had ruled that indirect purchasers could sue for treble damages. In re Western Liquid Asphalt Cases was the most notable example of this type of ruling. The Supreme Court in fact granted certiorari in Illinois Brick in order to "resolve a conflict among the courts of appeals on the question of whether the offensive use of pass-on authorized by the decision below is consistent with Hanover Shoe's restrictions on the defensive use of pass-on."[26]

---

[25] Philadelphia Housing Authority v. American Radiator and Standard Sanitary Corporation, 50 F.R.D. 13 (1970).

[26] 431 U.S. 720 at 728.

The positive rulings such as those in Western Liquid Asphalt would at the very best be a neutral influence on the willingness and ability of indirect purchasers to bring treble damage suits when compared to, say, a modified statute of limitations scheme. Under the latter rules, not only would the potential plaintiffs know they could sue, but they would acquire the exclusive right to sue and receive recovery in the event that plaintiffs above them in the chain of distribution did not sue. Therefore, the existence of circuits where indirect purchasers did not believe they had standing to sue would serve to bias downward the observed number or frequency of indirect purchaser suits. The same phenomenon would also make it difficult to apply a case by case approach in a single circuit, since all plaintiffs in that circuit would be governed by similar expectations of the success of their litigation.

(8) Endogenous Changes on Defendant's Side--The hypothetical regression result explained above which would produce an estimate of the probability of a direct purchaser suit given various market conditions under which price fixing takes place, cannot be blindly projected to produce an estimate of the scope of cases where deterrence would be lost under alternate rules of standing. We have seen above that even if the data were perfect, any measurement of direct (or indirect) purchaser suits would be biased due to the fact that we are making observations under one set of rules of standing and attempting to project them to fit an environment with different rules. This general proposition is equally true with respect to behavior on the defendant's side. Rational would-be price fixers are likely to alter their behavior in the face of obvious opportunities to avoid being sued. When making a decision as to whether or not to fix prices, potential price fixers will be concerned with the probability of

being sued. To the extent that this probability depends on the extent of injury of parties with legal standing, the composition of markets in which price fixing takes place is likely to change in the direction of markets where those who are seriously injured do not have legal standing to sue. In markets where only indirect purchasers are seriously injured, violators would be relatively well protected from suit and therefore could increase their price fixing dramatically without much fear of being brought to bar for their illegal acts. Thus, even if data were perfect and the other biases enumerated above did not exist, reliable evidence cannot be obtained to predict the state of future deterrence on the basis of past behavior when rules changes would enable potential defendants to alter the markets in which they fix prices in response to such rules changes.

III. Another Approach

While the above case by case "cross sectional" approach was seen to suffer numerous problems of data collection and yield biased results notwithstanding, a second approach is called for. Such a "time series" approach will ask the following question: What happened to pending cases shortly before and after June 9, 1977, the data of the Illinois Brick decision?

Prior to Illinois Brick, four possible combinations of parties could have been suing: direct purchasers only, (DP), indirect purchasers only, (IP), both direct and indirect purchasers, (DP, IP), and no one, (O). After Illinois Brick, direct purchasers only and no suits are the only possible combinations.[27] By examining changes in the composition of active

---

[27] This statement ignores the situation where indirect purchasers remain

plaintiffs suing in the same cases both before and after the Illinois Brick decision, we may avoid the most serious biases enumerated above. Direct purchaser behavior would be observed under the Illinois Brick rule directly, rather than inferring their probable behavior under a situation when they did not have exclusive standing to sue. Because our observations are single cases in process over a short time span, the ceteris paribus assumption is valid. That is, changes in the composition of the plaintiffs suing can be, at least in most instances, attributable to Illinois Brick itself. Moreover, endogenous changes in defendant's behavior are irrelevant.

The eight combinations of parties suing before and after Illinois Brick can be depicted as follows:

```
            Before                          After
         Illinois Brick                 Illinois Brick

    (1)  DP-------------------------------DP

    (2)  DP------------------------------- O

    (3)  IP-------------------------------DP

    (4)  IP------------------------------- O

    (5)  DP, IP---------------------------DP

    (6)  DP, IP--------------------------- O

    (7)  O -------------------------------DP

    (8)  O ------------------------------- O
```

The Illinois Brick court argued that the concentration of the ability to sue in the direct purchaser class would encourage direct purchaser suits.

---

in the litigation attempting to prove that one or more exceptions to the Illinois Brick rule applies. Such instances will be dealt with later.

The Court also argued that the necessity of having to prove that an overcharge had not been passed on and the possibility of having to share recovery with indirect purchasers would diminish direct purchaser suits. If this seemingly reasonable proposition has any empirical validity we should see direct purchasers filing new suits and/or joining ongoing litigation after Illinois Brick. If on the other hand, the court was wrong, or for one reason or another some unwillingness to sue their suppliers predominated, direct purchasers would remain out of active litigation even when they were handed an easy case.

In the above schema, of the eight possibilities listed, numbers (1) and (5) where direct purchasers were suing their suppliers both before and after Illinois Brick, would tell us very little about the differences in the propensity to sue of direct purchasers produced by Illinois Brick. Cases (2) and (6) where direct purchasers are suing before Illinois Brick but not afterward would be expected to be highly improbable, although if found would certainly cast doubt on the reasoning underlying Illinois Brick.[28] (3), (4), (7), and (8) then would be the interesting cases. (3) and (7) where direct purchasers step in after Illinois Brick would seem to indicate that the court's argument is correct.[29] (4) and (8) where direct purchasers do not participate as a result of Illinois Brick would appear to indicate that the "unwillingness to sue suppliers" argument wins out over the "concentration of the ability to sue in one party" argument.

---

[28] Possibility (6) might arise if direct purchasers initially stepped in only because indirect purchasers were suing. In such an instance they might drop out after Illinois Brick. Such an example, if found would certainly cast doubt on the Illinois Brick reasoning.

[29] Of course the possibility that these cases would have been brought even in the absence of Illinois Brick cannot be ruled out.

A natural source of information for such an approach would be the various state attorneys general. They are in a position to report first hand on the litigation experience falling under categories (3) and (4), since as a group they are very active in treble damage cases, almost exclusively as indirect purchasers. In addition, the state attorneys general are to some extent also knowledgable about categories (7) and (8) because in many instances they may have been in the process of preparing to file a case but did not do so precisely because of <u>Illinois Brick</u>.[30] Since the state attorneys general are theoretically capable of shedding light on all four of the interesting cases, they were chosen for survey. In addition, such a survey would help illuminate the general prevalence of direct purchaser suits. Such observations, however, are of secondary importance due to the biases inherent in any approach where endogenous changes in the behavior of both potential price fixers and potential plaintiffs are possible in response to changes in the rules of the game. This survey approach deals primarily not with the absolute number or frequency of direct purchaser suits, but with changes in such suits as exogenous parameters are changed.

There are numerous reasons why the state attorneys general would be a rich and important source of information. First, there would be a large but manageable number of data points and to the extent that many states are involved in the same case, duplicate data would exist for cross checking. Secondly, the attorneys general would be a valuable source of information where judgmental issues are concerned. Particularly where

---

[30] The same reasoning could be applied to the state attorneys general's knowledge of (5) and (6) and of (1) and (2) respectively. As indicated above, these two categories are not considered to be probable events.

small insignificant plaintiffs file treble damage suits, and are prepared to settle for trivial amounts, or where undeserving plaintiffs harass defendants, the attorneys general would be expected to be able to distinguish these instances from those of active plaintiff participation. Such discrimination would not be obvious from reading opinions or statistics on filings. Most importantly, as mentioned above, direct purchasers would be observed under the actual circumstances of a direct purchaser rule, not under alternative conditions where they may have to prove passing on or share recovery.

Surveys were mailed to all 50 state antitrust directors, who are typically assistant attorneys general. A copy of such survey is reprinted below in the text. Respondents were asked to answer one questionnaire for each market in which they were involved in a treble damage action on June 9, 1977, the date of the _Illinois Brick_ decision. In addition respondents were asked to answer questions concerning suits they would have filed but for _Illinois Brick_.

The first several questions serve to identify the industry in which price fixing was alleged both for the purposes of cross checking between states and also in order to make inferences about elasticities and other interesting parameters. The next several questions pertain to the direct purchaser role in antitrust enforcement. These questions seek to determine whether direct purchasers were active participants, whether they instigated the litigation or where passive followers, and whether they moved in after _Illinois Brick_. In each case approximate magnitudes of direct purchaser involvement are sought.

The next block of questions, beginning on page two of the questionnaire, are designed to determine whether these industries may fall

The following questions pertain to treble damage actions brought by your state, either as parens patriae or in your proprietary capacity, which were pending on June 9, 1977, the date of the Illinois Brick decision. The same questions are also appropriate if you were planning to file suit, but did not do so solely because of Illinois Brick. Please complete one copy of this questionnaire for each relevant case.

1) Who is (are) the defendant(s)?

2) What is the product market in which damages were alleged?

3) Were you (or the citizens of your state) direct or indirect purchasers of the alleged antitrust violator?

   ____ direct   ____ indirect   ____ other (please specify)

4) What good or service did you purchase?

5) What was the complaint?

   ____ price fixing   ____ monopolization   ____ other (please specify)

6) Approximately what percentage of direct purchasers filed suit? (Specify percent if possible)

   ____ most or all sued
   ____ some sued
   ____ none sued   about ____ % filed suit
   ____ don't know

7) Did any direct purchasers file before you did?

   ____ yes   ____ no   ____ don't know

8) If you were an indirect purchaser, what happened to your case after Illinois Brick?

   ____ thrown out of court
   ____ other (please specify)

9) Did any direct purchasers sue subsequent to June 9, 1977? Please specify percent if possible.

   ____ most or all sued
   ____ some sued   about ____ % filed suit
   ____ none sued
   ____ irrelevant question since most were already suing
   ____ other (please specify)

The following questions attempt to characterize the direct purchaser class.

10) Is the direct purchaser owned or controlled in any way - - - -

    by the defendant? ____ yes ____ no ____ don't know
    by its customer? ____ yes ____ no ____ don't know

    If so, in what manner?

11) Are you aware of the existence of a cost plus markup pricing system at the direct purchaser level?

    ____ cost plus   ____ not cost plus   ____ don't know

12) If you were an indirect purchaser, was the good altered in form between the time it was sold by the defendant and purchased by your state?

    ____ Yes, the original good was an input into my good (e.g., cement blocks in buildings).
    ____ Yes, the original good was a capital good (e.g., shoe machinery in shoes).
    ____ No, the good was not altered (direct purchaser a middleman or broker).
    ____ Other (please specify)

13) To your knowledge has the direct purchaser received a settlement or judgment from the defendant?

    ____ yes   ____ no   ____ still pending   ____ don't know

14) If yes, was the settlement obtained before *Illinois Brick*?

15) If yes (to 13)), how does this settlement/judgment compare in size to what your state was expecting?

16) If you were an indirect purchaser what is the approximate value of the overcharged item as a proportion of the value of the product you purchased?

17) Is the direct purchaser industry usually characterized by shortages?

    ____ yes   ____ no   ____ don't know

18) Is there anything unusual about this case or about the direct purchaser requiring comment?

19) Is there a written opinion in this case?

    ____ yes
    ____ no   citation _____
    ____ don't know   JPML # _____

within the "exceptions" of the Illinois Brick rule, that is ownership or control, or cost plus pricing. Of particular interest would be instances where the functional equivalent of these exceptions was present but proof would be nearly impossible. For example, cost plus pricing may exist in many industries, but if such pricing is not specified in a contract, indirect purchasers may not be permitted to sue.

In addition, the chacteristics of the price fixed good were requested, that is, whether it was a capital good (like Hanover Shoe), an input (like Illinois Brick), or the same good (the Oil Jobber Cases). This information might be useful in determining whether a rule should be devised which depends on the form in which the price fixed good reaches indirect purchasers. Finally the last questions are concerned with any judgments or settlements that have been paid out and how they would compare to what the states were expecting to receive. Such questions seek to determine the relative deterrence effect in such instances where direct purchasers and indirect purchasers have both sued.

Responses of some sort were received from 31 states, far more than expected. The quality of several of the responses, however, was extremely low. A few states wrote back either that they did not have antitrust departments or that they had not yet brought any treble damage suits. Two states indicated that they were not willing to answer the survey. In other instances the interesting questions, such as whether direct purchasers filed after Illinois Brick, were left blank. On many occasions, the respondents simply checked the blank "some sued," thus providing very little information. Little usable information was conveyed by this response because there was no way to know whether "some" meant 1 or 45 direct purchasers out of 50 possible firms suing.[31] In addition, there was no way to distinguish between serious litigants who were actively striving to obtain the entire value of their damages trebled and insignificant plaintiffs content with a recovery whose value was only a small fraction of the treble damages. In all, about a dozen states supplied information that was extremely useful, complete and unambiguous. In order to supplement this information and to clear up ambiguities concerning the roles of direct purchasers in particular cases, several state antitrust directors were telephoned as well.[32] These lengthy conversations were particularly useful in filling in gaps and removing ambiguities inherent in some written responses.

Although the sample of cases was small, the results were startlingly clear. Not only were direct purchasers not active plaintiffs in the vast majority of the cases, but there were no perceivable changes in direct purchaser behavior as a result of Illinois Brick. A much more detailed analysis is provided in the next section.

IV. Survey Results

There was considerable overlap in the responses of the several state antitrust directors. This was particularly true in instances such as the

---

[31]Admittedly, this ambiguity may have been a fault of the author and not of the respondent.

[32]The Special Assistant to the Chairman of the National Association of Attorneys General supplied me with the names of 12 states whose antitrust directors were particularly knowledgable and experienced on the issue of Illinois Brick. Of these 12, 7 had already responded to the survey. The remaining 5 were telephoned. By the third or fourth call significant diminishing returns set in. Not only were the cases discussed overlapping but their analyses of the effects of Illinois Brick were mutually consistent.

sugar litigation[33] where large classes of plaintiffs including numerous states have been consolidated for pretrial proceedings or trial by the Multidistrict Litigation Panel. In all about two dozen different cases were mentioned by the various states. After eliminating those in which insufficient information was available and those few instances in which the states sued only as direct purchasers, seventeen cases or clusters of cases remained. They are listed alphabetically by product in the first column of the table below.

The second column in the table indicates the names of the various states who gave substantive information on a case filed in a given industry against the same defendants. In several instances states mentioned which actions they had filed but gave no substantive information concerning direct purchaser activity. Such states are excluded from the table. The number of states gives a rough idea of the extent to which we can rely on the observation. An asterisk appears in this column next to the states where information was obtained by the various state antitrust directors in telephone calls. Both because those individuals interviewed were among the most knowledgable and active in treble damage cases and because there was virtually no possibility they could have misinterpreted my questions as presented orally, these observations should be given somewhat greater weight.

The third column indicates whether direct purchasers were suing before _Illinois Brick_. The next column indicates, where available, whether the direct purchasers either joined ongoing litigation or initiated new suits after (and presumably in response to) _Illinois Brick_.

---

[33] _In re Sugar Antitrust Litigation_, MDL #201.

TABLE 1. TREBLE DAMAGE CASES

Product	Number of Observations	Were Direct Purchasers Suing?	Sued After Illinois Brick?	If Not, Why Not?	Type of Good
Ampicillin (Semisynthetic Penicillin)	Alabama California Hawaii Minnesota Missouri* Ohio Oregon* Washington Wisconsin	No substantial suit by any direct purchaser	None at all	Very inelastic demand, cost plus pricing but not within Illinois Brick exception (one respondent noted shortages)	Same good
Armored Car	California* Hawaii New Jersey	Very few filed, received token settlements**	None	Control by supplier, too much risk	Same good
Bread	Montana	None sued	None		Same good
Cement	Arizona* California* Colorado Minnesota Missouri* Nebraska Washington	Very few if any ready mix companies (the direct purchasers) relatively few of first indirect purchaser level (contractors)	Very few	Very low derived elasticity in final product, financial control by cement companies, some shortages reported	Same good and input
Chickens	Alabama Delaware Florida Massachusetts Missouri* New Jersey Ohio	Many or most sued, settled for unknown magnitude	None after		Same good

TABLE 1 (continued)

Product	Number of Observations	Were Direct Purchasers Suing?	Sued After Illinois Brick?	If Not, Why Not?	Type of Good
Dairy	Arizona*	Small grocer sued as class representing all. Most opted out of litigation and did not sue themselves!	None		Same good
Electrical Wiring Devices	Minnesota (Many states reported that they would have filed but for Illinois Brick but gave little or no information)	Uncertain, probably few if any		Very low derived elasticity of demand	Purchased in buildings
Fertilizer	Alaska, Idaho, Oregon*, Washington	None at all	None	Some ownership and/or financial control alleged	Same good
Fine Paper	Arizona*, California*, Connecticut, Hawaii, Missouri*, New Jersey, Oregon*, Washington, Wisconsin	No direct purchasers at all, very few at first indirect purchaser level**	None after Illinois Brick	Ownership or control by paper manufacturers	Same good

204

TABLE 1(continued)

Product	Number of Observations	Were Direct Purchasers Suing?	Sued After Illinois Brick?	If Not, Why Not?	Type of Good
Liquid Asphalt	Alabama	No direct purchasers (other than state)	None after (state filed after)	Low elasticity, cost plus pricing system	Same good
Master Key	Alabama Arizona* Hawaii New Jersey	Very few if any	None (though statute of limitations may have run)	Very small derived elasticity	Input into buildings
Petroleum (Refined Products)	Arizona* California* Florida Oregon* Washington	None at all, the only plaintiffs were states (and one city)	None at all	Financial dependence on supplier, subject to lease termination	Same good
Plywood	Hawaii Oregon*	Very few if any	None after Illinois Brick	Fear of disturbing relationship with suppliers, some shortages reported	
Potash	Minnesota	Nationwide direct purchaser class sued and received settlement, magnitude unknown			

TABLE 1 (continued)

Product	Number of Observations	Were Direct Purchasers Suing?	Sued After Illinois Brick?	If Not, Why Not?	Type of Good
Sugar	Alabama California* Colorado Connecticut Delaware Georgia Massachusetts Missouri Minnesota Nevada Washington Wisconsin Oregon*	Surveys indicate that many or most direct purchasers suing in a large class action. However small firms with miniscule claims initiated litigation and important and large firms not active litigants		There is evidence that some firms may have known about conspiracy (Coca Cola)	Usually an input
Steel Rebar (Reinforcing Steel Bars)	Alabama Florida Oregon* Texas Washington	No substantial direct purchaser filed suit	None		Usually an input

*One state out of the several responding thought that most direct purchasers had sued.

The fifth column offers a rough guess as to the reasons why direct purchasers might not have sued (if they did not sue). The common answers seem to be control by suppliers, cost plus pricing and inelastic demands, and/or shortages in the industry. The final column indicates the form of the good as it was sold by direct purchasers, that is, whether is was a capital good, an input into the direct purchaser's good or the same good.

The principal substantive conclusion to be drawn from the results appearing in the table concerns the role of direct purchaser suits in private antitrust enforcement. Not only is the general level or frequency of direct purchaser suits quite low and therefore probably quite ineffective in deterring antitrust violators, but also there was no observable affect of Illinois Brick on the willingness to bring price fixing cases. In response to the second conclusion, one might argue that either (1) direct purchasers were already suing before Illinois Brick, (2) the statute of limitations had already run or settlements had already been arranged, or more probably, (3) that direct purchasers were deterred from entering because indirect purchasers sometimes remained in the litigation attempting to prove an exception to Illinois Brick. However, in only a very small proportion of instances were direct purchasers suing at all and in almost all instances the cases were very new. (Ampicillin and Master Key are two exceptions.) In many instances the indirect purchasers were thrown out of court. However, even if indirect purchasers had not been thrown out of court, but remained in the litigation attempting to prove an exception to the Illinois Brick rule, the results obtained would still be indicative of the true effects of Illinois Brick. This is true because there is no reason to believe that indirect purchasers would behave any differently in the future if Illinois Brick holds. Rather, they can be expected to continually attempt to prove the appropriateness of one of its exceptions. This conclusion must of course be weakened to the extent that indirect purchasers are remaining in the litigation only awaiting Congressional legislation overruling Illinois Brick. The survey was taken a sufficiently long period of time after Illinois Brick (14 months) for direct purchasers to prepare to sue. Surely if the "concentration of the ability to sue" argument had any validity we would have seen direct purchasers respond to Illinois Brick in at least one of the seventeen industries. The conclusion seems to follow that the Supreme Court's argument--that the exclusive ability to sue helps deterrence--while on its face reasonable, has little empirical validity.

The level or frequency of direct purchaser suits both before and after Illinois Brick is also unquestionably low. In only three cases did the initial surveys appear to indicate significant direct purchaser activity before Illinois Brick: chickens, sugar and potash. The sugar case is particularly illustrative, as it neatly displays the "weak plaintiff" suit. In the sugar industry a few small, almost insignificant, plaintiffs filed suit on behalf of a national class of direct sugar consumers. Two of these plaintiffs are Grandma's Cookies, and Mother's Cookies who filed suit on behalf of such giants as Coca Cola, General Mills and Pillsbury each of whom use enormous quantities of sugar. Rather than "opting out," these large firms remained passive members of the class. According to the antitrust directors of both California and Oregon, there is no doubt that Coca Cola and the other giants would increase their settlement by perhaps even an order of magnitude if they were to opt out and actively proceed with their own litigation.[34]

This "weak plaintiff" situation occurs repeatedly. According to Michael Spiegel, the Assistant Attorney General of California, in the Ampicillin case a couple of small drug stores filed suit on behalf of all drug stores and hospitals in the nation. The suit benefits lawyers and may very well be solicited by lawyers. Other plaintiffs named in the class action have no incentive to opt out of the litigation, for they cannot be harmed by the defendant if everyone else stays in. On the other hand, they apparently have no incentives to opt out in order to bring their own suit, perhaps because they are themselves benefiting from the conspiracy or that they do not want to risk possible deterioration of the quality of their relationships with their suppliers.

According to Spiegel another "sweetheart" deal occurred in the fine paper industry. Virtually all fine paper is sold directly to merchant houses who act as brokers for the paper. No merchant houses sued either before or after Illinois Brick, perhaps because they were owned or controlled by the paper manufacturers. In addition, treble damage suits by the first layer of indirect purchasers were infrequent. In one instance a fish market using paper to wrap its fish sued on behalf of many large firms in the "Fortune 500."[35] While such instances may appear as if a comprehensive set of direct purchasers is actively pursuing treble damages from the defendants, the true story is quite the opposite. The actual deterrence of antitrust violators is apt to be negligible when small plaintiffs, perhaps solicited by their lawyers, are willing to settle for token magnitudes.

---

[34] Conversation with Michael Speigel, California on 9/28/78 and with Kirk Johns of Oregon on 10/4/78.

[35] Conversation with Michael Spiegel, 9/28/78.

Chicken and potash were the other two instances of apparently significant direct purchaser activity. In potash there was but one observation. The state of Minnesota responded that at least one direct purchaser had sued but responded "don't know" when asked about the frequency of direct purchaser suits. In neither potash nor chicken was any information obtained about the "quality" of the plaintiff(s), so the "weak plaintiff" argument cannot be ruled out.

Not only was there no observable change in the propensity of direct purchasers to bring suit as a result of <u>Illinois Brick</u>, but for this sample of cases, the general level or frequency of direct purchaser suits was very low. Above we argued that a case by case approach which focuses on behavior before <u>Illinois Brick</u> might be inappropriate because of endogenous changes by both plaintiffs and defendants. Plaintiffs may be <u>more</u> likely to bring suit if they do not have to share recovery or prove passing on. On the other hand though, potential price fixers are likely to change the composition of markets in which price fixing takes place in the direction of markets in which direct purchasers are not seriously injured. Thus, with no <u>a priori</u> knowledge, the deterrence of antitrust violators could move in either direction! However, since we have just shown the first effect to be empirically inconsequential, it should be concluded that the existing frequency of direct purchaser suits,[36] low as it may be, would prove to be an <u>upper limit</u>, once price fixers respond to changes in situations in which they are not truly liable for their illegal actions. Although it must be conceded that the sample of cases in which the states were involved in treble damage litigation may itself be biased, the fact

---

[36] Frequency of suits refers to their proportion of total violations.

remains that at least for this sample, the upper limit of direct purchaser suits is uncomfortably low.

The principal reasons which appear to explain the reluctance of direct purchasers to sue their suppliers, ironically, are precisely those with which the Supreme Court was most concerned, cost plus pricing and ownership and control. However, the two exceptions to the Illinois Brick rule may be so narrowly drawn that a large fraction of instances in which there is _effective_ cost plus pricing or _effective_ control may not fall within these exceptions.

The Illinois Brick court indicated that an exception might be made "for a preexisting cost plus contract. In such a situation, the purchaser is insulated from any decrease in its sales as a result of attempting to pass on the overcharge, because its customer is committed to buying a fixed quantity regardless of price."[37] Thus, unless a contract is actually drawn up in which exact quantities are specified, the cost plus exception does not allow indirect purchasers to sue. In markets such as liquid asphalt or pharmaceuticals where a cost plus formula is admittedly used, but there is no _contract_, the exception may not be allowed.

Another important reason which appears to explain the reluctance of direct purchasers to sue is some kind of control exercised by the defendant upon the direct purchaser, often control through a financial arrangement. The Court in stating its ownership or control exception was not very specific. It said, "Another situation in which market forces have been superseded and the pass-on defense might be permitted is where the direct purchaser is owned or controlled by its customer."[38] Not only

---

[37] 431 U.S. 720, 736.

[38] 431 U.S. 720, 736 (footnote).

was the Court not specific in defining the meaning of ownership or control, but is specified control by a <u>customer</u> and not the potential defendant. It remains very unclear to what extent the ownership or control of the direct purchaser by its supplier will come within the exception to the <u>Illinois Brick</u> rule. Even in the extreme case where all forms of control, however minor, come under the exception, the results may not greatly benefit antitrust enforcement. Under such a scenario the <u>Illinois Brick</u> rule would be effectively nullified, but at a high price in terms of the administrative costs of proving "control." Thus, in cases where there is a question of ownership or control, little has been gained. Either the substantial deterrence of antitrust violators is lost or substantial administrative costs are added, depending on the leniency of the courts in interpreting this exception.

The last column of the table indicates the form of the good as purchased by the indirect purchaser. There was insufficient variety of responses to be able to make any conclusions about the dependence of the propensity of direct purchasers to sue on the use to which the price fixed good was put, that is, whether it was an input or remained unchanged. However, there is no positive evidence to lead to the conclusion that a rule should be devised to distinguish between these two categories. Similarly, there was not enough information provided on settlements in written or oral questions to be able to conclude anything of any significance.

Thus we are left with two conclusions. First, the <u>Illinois Brick</u> decision does not appear to produce significant changes in direct purchaser behavior. Secondly, at least for this sample of cases, the general frequency of direct purchaser suits, which was shown to put an upper limit on effective deterrence once violators were able to change their own behavior, is quite low. The next and final chapter will summarize the results obtained and suggest appropriate policy changes.

CHAPTER VII

CONCLUSION

This dissertation has examined the private antitrust enforcement mechanism in order to suggest policies to resolve the dilemma brought about by the Illinois Brick decision. The present chapter reviews the substantive conclusions of this study concerning both private antitrust enforcement in general and Illinois Brick in particular. It then suggests policy changes which are likely to have beneficial economic effects when judged by both the criteria of efficiency and compensation.

In the quest for optimal rules of standing for private antitrust cases involving chains of manufacturing and distribution we examined the private enforcement mechanism in Chapter II. There we saw antitrust enforcement to be a public good and proceeded to determine the efficient level of its provision. An efficient level of antitrust enforcement in the context of a general equilibrium model is set by the minimization of the welfare losses due to antitrust violations and the administrative costs of enforcement by all parties involved. Like many other public goods antitrust enforcement can be either publicly or privately provided. Before comparing the efficiency of public versus private enforcement, we examined the principal arguments of the most severe critics of the private enforcement mechanism. Here we concluded that the harshest criticisms of private antitrust enforcement --that it was subject to perverse incentives, harassment and overenforcement--were considerably less serious than critics had suggested. Public and private enforcement were then compared to determine which group would be the more efficient provider. The spillover effects between public and private enforcement indicated that antitrust enforcement provided by both the public and the private sector was superior to the enforcement provided by either sector alone. Since optimal provision of antitrust enforcement was determined to require the participation of the private sector, including states, we were then in a position to determine which private parties, that is direct or indirect purchasers or both, should be afforded legal standing to sue antitrust violators.

In deciding whether the <u>Illinois Brick</u> decision or some other rule of standing best satisfies the goals of antitrust enforcement, it would be wise to keep explicit exactly what these goals are. In this dissertation, we have framed these goals in terms of efficiency and compensation. Since efficient enforcement is defined as minimizing the welfare losses due to undeterred violations plus the costs of enforcement, there is both a deterrence component and an administrative cost component to efficiency. A chapter each was devoted to compensation, to the administrative costs of enforcement, and of course to the deterrence of antitrust violators.

Before reviewing the substantive conclusions of these three chapters it should be noted that there are tradeoffs among these three goals. Compensation is not itself a costless goal, rather social costs are incurred in administering policies which fairly and adequately compensate the victims of antitrust violations. This is particularly true in the satisfaction of notice requirements and in the computations of individual damages in class action suits, and in the proof of passing on in chain of distribution cases. Here the furtherance of the goal of compensation is achieved at the expense of efficient enforcement.

Similarly, it was seen in Chapter II that the two components of efficiency, deterrence and the costs of enforcement, may be negatively related. More specifically, at the welfare maximum, in order to reduce the number and hence costs of antitrust violations, the costs of suit must increase. Even if we are not at the point of optimal enforcement, provided that the violation curve does not move, any policy changes which serves to change plaintiff's behavior will incur increasing welfare losses due to undeterred violations in order to cut enforcement costs, or incur increased costs of enforcement in order to reduce the number of antitrust violations.

There may not be a tradeoff between the third pair of goals, deterrence and compensation. Instead deterrence and compensation may be positively related in the sense that further deterrence of antitrust violators will reduce the number of uncompensated victims of antitrust violations, ceteris paribus. These relationships between the three goals of antitrust enforcement must be kept in mind when examining the implications of each separate goal.

In Chapter III we examined the incidence of an overcharge of a price fixed good in a chain of manufacturing or distribution. This was accomplished by examining the implications of various partial equilibrium models of incidence while demand elasticity, market structure, cost conditions, the elasticity of substitution and other variables were allowed to vary.

When the results of these models were applied to a set of recent price fixing cases brought by the Department of Justice, we concluded that most or all of the overcharge was passed on by the direct purchasers, especially in the long run. The implications of this conclusion are clearly that from the perspective of proper compensation, indirect purchasers should be allowed to bring treble damage actions against antitrust violators.

Chapter V examined the question of the administrative costs of enforcement. Both the issues of the increasing complexity and unmanageability of litigation and of multiple liability were discussed. Here we reasoned that although *Illinois Brick* would in fact eliminate some of the additional costs of enforcement such as those of proving passing on, and of multiparty litigation, that this rule would be too blunt an instrument for tackling the problem of enforcement costs. Instead, certain reforms of class action procedures and antitrust trials would probably produce equivalent results at less social cost. The administrative costs of enforcement which would remain after these reforms had been implemented, are the relevant costs to be compared in deciding between alternative standing rules.

Multiple liability, although a legitimate cost to society, is relatively easy to avoid using specified procedural devices, and furthermore has been empirically unimportant. Even if multiple liability were to occur more frequently in the future, the gains brought about by reducing the probability that multiple liability will occur must be weighed against the sacrifices incurred in the spheres of deterrence and compensation.

Chapter VI examined the question of deterrence, that is, who sues the price fixer. In this chapter evidence from individual cases was presented to demonstrate that in a considerable number of instances direct purchasers did not sue their suppliers. This case by case approach was not pursued further because serious biases are inevitably introduced. Rather, instead of observing the numbers of actual cases brought by direct purchasers, the changes (if any) in the behavior of these parties during a period in which the rules of standing had changed were examined. Through a survey of the fifty state antitrust directors, the propensity of direct purchasers to sue their suppliers before and after Illinois Brick was observed. Although the sample was relatively small and perhaps biased in some unknown fashion, the results were clear. No significant changes in the propensity of direct purchasers to sue their suppliers was obvious as a result of Illinois Brick. In contrast to direct purchaser inactivity, the states were seen to be very active in bringing treble damage suits. Although little can be concluded about private[1] indirect purchaser activity, the absence of direct purchaser plaintiffs in most instances indicates that the deterrence of antitrust violators would be better served by allowing indirect purchasers to sue and collect treble damages, at least where direct purchasers are not suing.

In the course of our discussions we were able to make two interim conclusions. First, that regardless of other rules of standing, the states should be allowed to sue antitrust violators even when they are indirect purchasers. Secondly, that there is at least one set of standing rules, one which utilizes a modified statute of limitations, which strictly dominates Illinois Brick; therefore, Illinois Brick should be overturned. The first conclusion, that the states should be afforded standing to sue as indirect purchasers, was reached by considering the effect of the addition of

---

[1] Although private antitrust enforcement is usually defined to include state enforcement, for the purposes of this chapter private enforcement will henceforth refer only to non-state enforcement unless otherwise stated.

state enforcement on each of the three enunciated goals. State enforcement clearly promotes both the deterrence and the compensation goals. In addition, due to various possible cost savings, it is a considerably more efficient means than private enforcement to enforce the antitrust laws. Since it promotes both deterrence and compensation and is in some sense an administrative cost bargain, states should be permitted to sue both as direct and indirect purchasers.

The second interim conclusion concerns one alternative to overrule Illinois Brick. A proposal was described in Chapter IV to amend the statute of limitations to sequentially allow direct and indirect purchasers the exclusive right to sue antitrust violators, without having to prove passing on. This proposal preserves all the advantages of Illinois Brick and in addition eliminates some of its disadvantages. Therefore, the Illinois Brick rule is strictly dominated by this strategy, and hence should be replaced by either this proposal or a superior one if it exists.

We are now left with four alternative sets of rules to replace Illinois Brick:

(1) The modified statute of limitations proposal,

(2) The amendment of the Clayton Act to allow only the states to sue as indirect purchasers,

(3) The overruling of both Hanover Shoe and Illinois Brick, or

(4) The overruling of Illinois Brick alone.[2]

---

[2] A fifth alternative mentioned in Chapter IV, which involves distinguishing between direct purchasers who "consume" the price fixed good in their own production processes and those who pass on such goods in unchanged form, seems to have little empirical support and therefore will not be discussed further.

Our task is to choose between these four alternatives based on the criteria of the extent to which each satisfies the goals of compensation, the minimization of enforcement costs and the deterrence of antitrust violators. This choice will be made by comparing the four alternatives pairwise or by sequentially asking these three questions:

(1) If we allow private indirect purchasers to sue by overruling *Illinois* *Brick*, should we also overrule *Hanover* *Shoe* as well? (i.e. does (3) dominate (4)?)

(2) Should parties other than states be allowed to sue as indirect purchasers? (i.e. do (3) and (4) dominate (2)?)

(3) Is the arbitrary statute of limitations scheme to be preferred to its best alternative, a discretionary scheme which uses more information but incurs costs in doing so? (i.e. does (1) dominate the rest?)

Provided that we choose to allow indirect purchasers other than states to sue antitrust violators, the single benefit of overruling the *Hanover* *Shoe* decision as well as *Illinois* *Brick* is that it lessens the chance of multiple liability. Multiple liability can only occur if direct and indirect purchasers sue in two different courts or at two (or more) different times and both determinations on the question of passing on go against the defendant. In the event that the direct purchaser does pass on the overcharge (the usual case), the indirect purchaser's chances of proving passing on is not likely to vary according to whether or not *Hanover* *Shoe* is overruled. Thus the question of multiple liability hinges on whether the direct purchaser can also recover damages. If *Hanover* *Shoe* is not overruled, direct purchasers in another courtroom may be able to collect treble damages since the defendant will not be allowed the passing on defense.

On the other hand, if Hanover Shoe is overruled, such collection will be considerably less likely due to the likelihood that the defendant will be able to prove that the overcharge was passed on.

Now let's consider the advantage of not overturning Hanover Shoe. This consists solely of the increased deterrence of antitrust violators. One of the reasons the Hanover Shoe court rejected the passing on defense was that in some instances,

> those who violate the antitrust laws by price fixing or monopolizing would retain the fruits of their illegality, because no one was available who would bring suit against them. Treble damage actions, the importance of which the court has many times emphasized, would be substantially reduced in effectiveness.[3]

In other words where the defendants were successful in their passing-on defense, and no indirect purchasers were available to sue, the defendants would retain their ill gotten profits. In deciding whether or not to overturn Hanover Shoe along with Illinois Brick, there are two relevant criteria to be considered: the costs and likelihood of multiple liability and the costs and likelihood of situations where the direct purchaser can't prove that he absorbed the overcharge but there are no indirect purchasers willing to bring suit.

We have seen above that multiple liability is empirically inconsequential. However, even if it were to occur more frequently in the future, less drastic means than overruling Hanover Shoe are available. From the point of view of deterrence, it does not matter to whom the defendant pays treble damages. Furthermore, it should be of no consequence to him which party actually absorbs the overcharge and receives the damages. For this

---

[3] Hanover Shoe v. United Shoe Machinery, 392 U.S. 481, 494.

reason a hybrid remedy is possible which preserves Hanover Shoe and at the same time eliminates multiple liability.

In order to eliminate the possibility of multiple liability, all parties could be forced to sue at once, perhaps in response to a notice of the first suit. The defendant would then be tried only on the issues of liability and extent of damages. Then the various plaintiffs would decide among themselves, by trial or settlement, how to divide up the total damages. In the event that only one level sues, be it direct or indirect, the passing on issue need not arise. The single party suing would have automatic recovery once the violation and its magnitude were proved. Even if the wrong party were compensated, this is still beneficial from the perspective of deterrence. From this perspective, it is better to give a windfall payment to an undeserving plaintiff then to allow it to remain in the hands of the defendant. In sum, the deterrence value of Hanover Shoe can be preserved while at the same time avoiding the pitfall of multiple liability if all parties are required to sue at once. Therefore, provided that private parties are permitted to sue as indirect purchasers, Hanover Shoe should be retained with the minor alternation just suggested.

Now that we have decided that only Illinois Brick should be overruled, assuming that we allow all private parties to sue as indirect purchasers, we must go back one step and examine the implications of this assumption by addressing question (2) above. Should only states be allowed to sue antitrust violators as indirect purchasers or should this right be extended to all private parties? In Chapter II we examined the conditions under which the addition of parties to the number of possible plaintiffs with legal standing would make antitrust enforcement more efficient. The reduced number of violations times the appropriate cost to society per violation must be weighed against the increased total costs of enforcement. While the true magnitudes of these variables are impossible to judge, a few observations are appropriate. First, when asked the question of whether much would be lost in terms of the deterrence of antitrust violators if only states were allowed to sue, the antitrust directors questioned tended to reply that the states would be a wholly inadequate substitute for all private parites. While the states are generally active in a multitude of important treble damage cases at any given time, in others they are merely passive participants relying on the hard work done by private firms. Secondly, from the standpoint of compensation, it is clearly superior to allow private parties to sue as indirect purchasers both because a greater number of total suits can be brought and also because states are not <u>required</u> to compensate individual victims when they sue as <u>parens patriae</u>. The administrative cost question is unclear. We argued above that states are probably lower cost litigators than other private parties. Therefore, the addition of private parties to the list of indirect purchaser plaintiffs would necessarily raise the costs per suit, due both to the relative inefficiency of private suits and to the additional costs of multiparty litigation. However, if class actions are streamlined as recently proposed by the Carter administration, many of the cost saving measures now possible in state suits would also be possible in other private suits.

It is somewhat hazardous to choose between the two alternatives at hand. However, considering the clear advantages of private indirect purchaser suits from the perspective of both deterrence and compensation, and the likelihood that the administrative costs of enforcement could be reduced considerably by reform legislation, it is probably correct to say that society would be better off by allowing all indirect purchasers to sue antitrust violators.

The final question which must be addressed is whether the best discretionary rule of standing, that <u>all</u> indirect purchasers be permitted to sue antitrust violators and that <u>Hanover Shoe</u> should remain law, is to be preferred to the arbitrary rule enunciated above, the modified statute of limitations plan. The two schemes are actually quite similar. From the perspective of deterrence, each proposal provides a generous opportunity for <u>some</u> party to sue the antitrust violator. Under the discretionary rule, where <u>Illinois Brick</u> is overruled, no proof of passing on would be necessary <u>unless</u> more than one level of purchasers is suing. Therefore, it is highly unlikely that the necessity of having to prove passing on would deter <u>all</u> parties from suing. This is especially true since we saw in Chapter VI that the concentration of the right to sue in a single class does not appear to influence the propensity to sue. Therefore, from the standpoint of deterrence both schemes perform quite well.

In terms of compensation, overturning <u>Illinois Brick</u> would clearly be superior. In the event that only one class of purchasers sues in each case, the results would be identical. But where both levels desire to sue, the statute of limitations scheme would compensate the direct purchaser only, where the discretionary scheme would allow the indirect purchaser an opportunity to obtain his rightful share.

The administrative cost criterion favors the statute of limitations scheme somewhat. However, since the cost of proving passing on would occur <u>only</u> when more than one class of purchasers sues, and since plaintiffs have shown remarkable adroitness in apportioning damages when the defendant was not involved, these additional costs incurred under the discretionary scheme may be very small.

Because the statute of limitations proposal was seen in Chapter IV to strictly dominate Illinois Brick, either this scheme or the remaining alternative, that of allowing all private parties to sue as indirect purchasers without overturning Hanover Shoe, should be chosen to replace the Illinois Brick rule. However, since the two proposals are roughly equivalent by the criterion of deterrence, but the statute of limitations scheme falls short on compensation and is superior on administrative costs, it is difficult to make a clear choice between them on these grounds alone. Any choice between these two rules, therefore, would be somewhat daring and speculative. However, if a choice between the two must be made, it would probably be better to avoid the arbitrariness of the statute of limitations scheme, an arbitrariness also present with the Illinois Brick rule. For this reason, it should be concluded that in the interests of furthering the efficiency and compensation objectives of the antitrust laws, Illinois Brick alone should be legislatively overruled by Congress to allow all indirect purchasers to sue antitrust violators.

BIBLIOGRAPHY

Administrative Office of the U.S. Courts, Annual Report, 1976, 1977.

American Bar Association, Section of Antitrust Law, Antitrust Law Developments, 1975.

Anonymous, "Mangano and Ultimate-Consumer Standing: The Misuse of the Hanover Doctrine," 72 Columbia Law Review (February 1972): 394-414.

Babb, Steven, "The Effect of Hanover Shoe on the Offensive Use of the Passing-On Doctrine," 46 Southern California Law Review (December 1972): 98-116.

Berger, Daniel, and Roger Bernstein, "An Analytical Framework for Antitrust Standing," 86 Yale Law Journal (April 1977): 809-883

Bork, Robert, The Antitrust Paradox. New York: Basic Books, 1978.

Bureau of National Affairs, Antitrust and Trade Regulation Reporter, Washington, D.C., various issues.

Commerce Clearing House, Trade Regulation Reporter, Chicago, various issues.

Elzinga, Kenneth, and William Breit, The Antitrust Penalties. New Haven: Yale University Press, 1976.

Erickson, Walter, "The Profitability of Violating the Antitrust Laws: Dissolution and Treble Damages in Private Antitrust?" 5 Antitrust Law and Economics Review (Summer 1972): 101-118.

Ferguson, C. E., The Neoclassical Theory of Production and Distribution. Cambridge: Cambridge University Press, 1971.

Handler, Milton, and Michael Blechman, "Antitrust and the Consumer Interest: The Fallacy of Parens Patriae and a Suggested New Approach," 85 Yale Law Journal (April 1976): 626-676.

Hay, George, and Daniel Kelly, "An Empirical Survey of Price Fixing Conspiracies," 17 Journal of Law and Economics (April 1974): 13-38.

Kinter, Earl; Joseph Griffin; and David Goldston, "The Hart-Scott-Rodino Antitrust Improvements Act of 1976: An Analysis," 46 George Washington Law Review (November 1977): 1-33.

Legal Times of Washington, 27 November 1978.

McGuire, Bartlett, "The Passing on Defense and the Right of Remote Purchasers to Recover Treble Damages under Hanover Shoe," 33 University of Pittsburgh Law Review (Winter 1971): 177-203.

New York Times, 30 September 1977.

Pollock, Earl, "Automatic Treble Damages and the Passing on Defense: The Hanover Shoe Decision," 13 Antitrust Bulletin (Winter 1968): 1183-1222.

Posner, Richard, Antitrust Law: An Economic Perspective. Chicago: University of Chicago Press, 1976.

_____, Economic Analysis of the Law. Boston: Little Brown & Co., 1972.

_____, "A Statistical Study of Antitrust Enforcement," 13 Journal of Law and Economics (October 1970): 365-419.

Schaeffer, Elmer, "Passing-On Theory in Antitrust Treble Damage Actions; An Economic and Legal Analysis," 16 William and Mary Law Review (Summer 1975): 883-936.

Scherer, Frederick, Industrial Market Structure and Economic Performance. Chicago: Rand McNally, 1970.

Stigler, George, A Theory of Price. New York: Macmillan, 1966.

U.S. Congress, House, Committee on the Judiciary, Effective Enforcement of the Antitrust Laws, Hearings before the Subcommittee on Monopolies and Commercial Law of the Committee on the Judiciary on H.R. 8359. 95th Cong., 1st sess., 1977.

U.S. Congress, Senate, Committee on the Judiciary, Fair and Effective Enforcement of the Antitrust Laws, S. 1874, Hearings before the Subcommittee on Antitrust and Monopoly of the Senate Judiciary Committee on S. 1874. 95th Cong., 1st sess., 1977.

Wheeler, Malcolm, "Antitrust Treble Damage Actions: Do They Work?" 61 California Law Review (December 1973): 1319-1352.

Weaver, Suzanne, The Decision to Prosecute: Organization and Public Policy in the Antitrust Division. Cambridge: M.I.T. Press, 1977.

TABLE OF CASES*

(1) *Bigelow v. RKO Radio Pictures*, 327 U.S. 251 (1946).

(2) *Boshes v. General Motors*, 59 F.R.D. 589 (N.D. Ill. 1973).

(3) *Brunswick Corp. v. Pueblo Bowl-O-Mat, Inc.*, 429 U.S. 477 (1977).

(4) *California v. Frito Lay*, 474 F. 2d 744 (9th Cir. 1973), *cert. denied* 412 U.S. 908 (1973).

(5) *FTC v. Fred Meyer*, 390 U.S. 341 (1968).

(6) *In re Gypsum Cases*, 386 F. Supp. 959 (1974).

(7) *Hanover Shoe v. United Shoe Machinery*, 392 U.S. 481 (1968).

(8) *Hawaii v. Standard Oil Co.*, 405 U.S. 251 (1972).

(9) *Illinois Brick v. State of Illinois*, 431 U.S. 720 (1977).

(10) *In re Master Key Antitrust Litigation*, 1973-2 Trade Cas. 74,680 (D.C. Conn. 1973).

(11) *Ohio Valley Electric Co. v. General Electric*, 244 F. Supp. 914 (S.D.N.Y. 1965).

(12) *Perkins v. Standard Oil*, 395 U.S. 642 (1969).

(13) *Perma Life Mufflers Inc. v. International Parts Co.*, 392 U.S. 134 (1968).

(14) *Philadelphia Housing Authority v. American Radiator and Standard Sanitary Corporation*, 50 F.R.D. 13 (E.D. Pa. 1970).

(15) *Radovich v. National Football League*, 352 U.S. 445 (1957).

(16) *Twin Ports Oil Co. v. Pure Oil Co.*, 119 F. 2d 747 (8th Cir. 1941), *cert. denied*, 314 U.S. 644 (1941).

(17) *West Virginia v. Charles Pfizer & Co.*, 440 F. 2d 1079 (2d Cir. 1971).

(18) *In re Western Liquid Asphalt Cases*, 487 F. 2d 191 (9th Cir. 1973), *cert. denied*, 415 U.S. 919 (1974).

---

*The cases in this table consist only of those for which written opinions are cited.